普通高等学校"十四五"规划英语实践实训数字化精品教材

英语语言实践教程

A Practical Coursebook on English Language Proficiency

主　编：蓝建青　贺　玲

编　者：赵　丹　王丽峰　张莹莹　阮广红
　　　　陈　媛　赵　辉

华中科技大学出版社
http://press.hust.edu.cn
中国·武汉

图书在版编目(CIP)数据

英语语言实践教程/蓝建青,贺玲主编. —武汉:华中科技大学出版社,2023.8
ISBN 978-7-5680-9941-7

Ⅰ.①英… Ⅱ.①蓝… ②贺… Ⅲ.①英语-教材 Ⅳ.①H319.39

中国国家版本馆 CIP 数据核字(2023)第 157794 号

英语语言实践教程
Yingyu Yuyan Shijian Jiaocheng

蓝建青 贺 玲 主编

策划编辑：周晓方 宋 焱	
责任编辑：刘 平	
封面设计：原色设计	
责任监印：周治超	
出版发行：华中科技大学出版社(中国•武汉)	电话：(027)81321913
武汉市东湖新技术开发区华工科技园	邮编：430223
录　　排：华中科技大学出版社美编室	
印　　刷：武汉市籍缘印刷厂	
开　　本：787mm×1092mm　1/16	
印　　张：16	
字　　数：382 千字	
版　　次：2023 年 8 月第 1 版第 1 次印刷	
定　　价：49.80 元	

本书若有印装质量问题,请向出版社营销中心调换
全国免费服务热线：400-6679-118　竭诚为您服务
版权所有　侵权必究

前言
Preface

改革开放以来,我国高等教育蓬勃发展,毛入学率显著上升,高等教育从精英教育走向大众教育。2021年3月,习近平总书记考察福建闽江学院时指出:"社会需要的人才是金字塔形的。高校不仅要培养研究型人才,也要树立应用型办学理念,培养青年一代适应社会需要的技能。"应用型本科高校占据我国本科院校的"半壁江山"。2014年以来,国家引导了一批本科院校向应用型高校发展,党和国家出台了一系列政策措施不断推进应用型本科高校的发展。在全面建设社会主义现代化国家新征程上,应用型高校外语专业应紧紧围绕服务国家、服务地方的办学方向,全面贯彻党的教育方针,落实立德树人根本任务,培养高素质、应用型外语人才。

2018年,教育部颁布《普通高等学校本科专业类教学质量国家标准(外国语言文学类)》;2020年,教育部高等学校外国语言文学类专业教学指导委员会英语专业教学指导分委员会颁布了《普通高等学校本科外国语言文学类专业教学指南》。这两个文件指导了我校2021版英语、商务英语专业培养方案的制定。《普通高等学校本科外国语言文学类专业教学指南》要求英语类专业学生具有扎实的英语语言基本功,良好的人文素养、中国情怀与国际视野,而应用型高校多类型、多规格的生源对学生培养质量带来较大压力。为此,经过慎重思考,我们尝试在综合性实践环节开设语言实践类课程,通过语言实践如篇章背诵、经典文本阅读、篇章听写等教学活动,提升学生的英语语言能力。经过两年的教学实践,效果明显,因此,我们将试用的《英语语言实践手册》1—4册进行重新整理,编成《英语语言实践教程》。

《英语语言实践教程》共分七个部分,分别为 Selected Essays, Vocabulary Building, Selected Readings, Passage Dictation, Mini-Lectures, Movie Clip Dubbing 和 Theatrical Performance。

第一部分为 Selected Essays。该部分精选32篇文章,其中包括学生耳熟能详的罗素(Bertrand Russell)、梭罗(Henry David Thoreau)、培根(Francis Bacon)、劳伦斯(D. H. Lawrence)等蜚声中外的英语文学作家的经典名篇,希冀学生在语言实践中培养人文精神,陶冶情操。同时,我们从《习近平谈治国理政》英文版中精选了7篇文章供学生背诵,让学生熟悉中国式现代化的表述,厚植中国情怀,将当代中国故事讲给世界听。

背诵课文（learning text by heart）需要反复诵读，直至一字不差地背出来或者默写出来。课文背诵是英语语言学习行之有效的方法。Sinclair（1991）和 Skehan（1998）等人认为语言具有两重性，即语言既是一个以语法为基础的可分析的系统，又是一个以记忆为基础的公式化的系统。丁言仁（2008）通过对三名在全国性英语演讲和辩论比赛中获奖的英语专业学生进行访谈，得出结论："对我最有用的方法是背书"。丁言仁、戚焱（2001）对南京大学外国语学院英语专业 84 名学生进行了调查，认为熟读和背诵课文有助于提高外语水平。

第二部分为 Vocabulary Building。本教程列出 32 个 word list。每个 list 中列出了 100 个重要单词，授课教师可以根据教学实际，安排词汇听写任务。在整个语言学习过程中，词汇学习非常重要。人们常以砖块和房子来比喻词汇和语言的关系，离开词汇，语言就失去了实际意义。英国著名语言学家 D. A. Wilkins 曾说："没有语法，很多东西无法传递；没有词汇，则任何东西都无法传递。"词汇学习伴随着人的一生。同时词汇表达内容、概念，所以，词汇反映人类对世界的认识。词汇量的大小直接影响听说读写各项能力的发展。教程虽然列出了重点词汇，但是英语类专业学生个体差异较大，词汇学习策略不尽相同，教师词汇呈现策略也不相同，教师和学生在使用时需要根据学生的学习情况，因材施教，提高学生英语词汇习得质量。

第三部分是 Selected Readings。教程根据教学指南的要求，精选了十六部作品，从 read to know, read to reason 和 read to create 等三个方面设计了练习题。教师可以根据学生实际情况，要求学生从不同的视角、不同的层面对文本进行阅读和思考。read to know 部分要求学生通过阅读，理解文本的背景、主要人物、性格特征等基本信息。read to reason 部分要求学生根据阅读内容进行推理和总结，较前一层次的要求有所提升。read to create 部分要求学生根据阅读内容中的某一个方面进行写作，需要生产具有创造性的内容。

英语类专业的人文属性已经成为教育界的共识。传统的英语类专业课程教学往往重视语言技能的训练，忽视了人文通识教育（liberal education）的使命。经典阅读不可或缺，教程提倡在经典阅读中一方面提高语言技能，培养英语语言能力，同时，通过文本细读，展开批判性研讨、批判性写作，形成学习共同体（Learning Community），提升学生独立思考、理性判断的能力，使学生人格得以成长。基于此，教程设置的问题从三个层次对学生提出要求，在进行文本细读的基础上，进行深度思考、推理、欣赏，达到布鲁姆-安德森认知能力模型中的"应用、分析、评价、创造"高阶能力，提升批判性思维能力。

第四部分和第五部分分别是 Passage Dictation 和 Mini-Lectures。所选内容根据原汁原味的语言材料进行改写，按照英语专业基础阶段考试（TEM4）的标准，邀请来自英语国家的人士进行录音。希冀通过大量的练习，提升学生的语言综合运用能力。这两个部分是英语专业基础阶段考试（TEM4）要求的内容，测试接收性（听）与产出性（写）语言技能，即听力理解能力、拼写熟练程度和正确运用标点符号的能力。事实上，在篇章听写和讲座测试中，既考查学生的信息获取能力，也考查学生的信息加工能力，还考查他们英语思维习惯、语篇交际功能、短时记忆能力等。这两部分测试是对听者听力、理解力和记忆能力的综合考查。

第六部分和第七部分是 Movie Clip Dubbing 和 Theatrical Performance。此处精选著名的英语电影片段和戏剧片段，以音频或视频的方式呈现，供学生进行模仿和表演。授课教师可根据教学实际，通过教学设计，让学生熟悉标准，通过不断的模仿、练习，最终以音频、视频或者表演的形式表现出来。英语类专业学生语音、语调教学是痛点之一，由于各种原因，有一部分学生的发音会带有地方特色口音，或对英语升降调把握欠佳，对习惯性发音（连读、不完全爆破等）掌握不住。将英语原声电影引入，组织学生进行配音，既能改善学生的语音、语调，又能增加词汇量，提高对句子的理解能力。戏剧是文学体裁之一，是通过舞台说明、台词及人物表演来体现人物性格及塑造人物形象的。戏剧表演可以调动学生学习英语的积极性和主动性，更好地帮助学生理解语言、灵活地运用语言，同时，学生的个人意识和团体协作精神也得到和谐发展。

本教程由蓝建青、贺玲担任主编，夏胜武主审。蓝建青负责总体设计、全书体例编写，并与贺玲负责统稿。本书各部分编写人员如下：Selected Essays（蓝建青、赵辉），Vocabulary Building（王丽峰、赵丹），Selected Readings（蓝建青、赵丹），Passage Dictation（张莹莹），Mini-Lectures（贺玲、王丽峰），Movie Clip Dubbing（阮广红），Theatrical Performance（陈媛）。

本教程主要面向英语类专业（英语专业、商务英语专业、翻译专业）本科、专科学生。

本教程选材来源在"参考文献"中列出，在此谨向文献的原作者表示衷心的感谢。

本教材的编写始终得到外国语学院院长曹曼教授的大力支持和帮助，得到华中科技大学出版社的鼎力支持，我们在此表示诚挚的谢意。

由于编者水平有限，错误在所难免。对于本书的纰漏之处，编者期望各位专家学者和读者不吝赐教，使我们能够及时改进。

编者谨识
2023 年 6 月

目录 Contents

Part One   Selected Essays   /1

Part Two   Vocabulary Building   /48

Part Three   Selected Readings   /173

Part Four   Passage Dictation   /185

Part Five   Mini-Lectures   /191

Part Six   Movie Clip Dubbing   /205

Part Seven   Theatrical Performance   /230

参考文献   /244

Part One
Selected Essays

Passage

Youth is not a time of life; it is a state of mind; it is not a matter of rosy cheeks, red lips and supple³ knees; it is a matter of the will, a quality of the imagination, a vigor of the emotions; it is the freshness of the deep springs of life.

Youth means a temperamental predominance of courage over timidity of the appetite, for adventure over the love of ease. This often exists in a man of sixty more than a boy of twenty. Nobody grows old merely by a number of years. We grow old by deserting our ideals.⁴

Years may wrinkle the skin, but to give up enthusiasm wrinkles the soul.⁵ Worry, fear, self-distrust bows the heart and turns the spirit back to dust.

Whether sixty or sixteen, there is in every human being's heart the lure of wonder, the unfailing childlike appetite of what's next, and the joy of the game of living. In the center of your heart and my heart there is a wireless station; so long as it receives messages of beauty, hope, cheer, courage and power from men and from the infinite, so long are you young.

When the aerials are down⁶, and your spirit is covered with snows of cynicism⁷ and the ice of pessimism, then you are grown old, even at twenty, but as long as your aerials are up, to catch the waves of optimism, there is hope you may die young at eighty.

Notes

1. This passage is published by *Reader's Digest* in 1945.

2. Samuel Ullman (April 13, 1840—March 21, 1924) was an American businessman, poet, humanitarian, and religious leader. He is best known today for this "Youth".

3. supple: A supple object or material bends or changes shape easily without cracking or breaking.

4. Nobody grows old merely by a number of years. We grow old by deserting our ideals: 年岁有加,并非垂老;理想丢弃,方堕暮年 (translated by Wang Zuoliang).

5. Years may wrinkle the skin, but to give up enthusiasm wrinkles the soul: Our body may change with time going by, but we can keep our soul young by keeping our enthusiasm towards life. 岁月悠悠,衰微只及肌肤;热忱抛却,颓废必至灵魂 (translated by Wang Zuoliang).

6. When the aerials of the wireless station in your heart are down, you can no longer receive messages which keeps you young.

7. cynicism: the belief that people always act selfishly.

Passage 2

Thoughts in a Grave Yard[1]

Joseph Addison[2]

When I look upon the tombs of the great, every emotion of envy dies in me; when I read the epitaphs[3] of the beautiful, every inordinate desire goes out; when I meet with the grief of parents upon a tombstone, my heart melts with compassion; when I see the tomb of the parents themselves, I consider the vanity of grieving for those whom we must quickly follow: when I see kings lying by those who deposed[4] them, when I consider rival wits placed side by side, or the holy men that divided the world with their contests and disputes, I reflect with sorrow and astonishment on the little competitions, factions, and debates of mankind[5]. When I read the several dates of the tombs, of some that died yesterday, and some six hundred years ago, I consider that great day when we shall all of us be contemporaries, and make our appearance together.

Part One Selected Essays

 Notes

1. This passage is an extract from "Thoughts in Westminster Abbey" published by *The Spectator* in 1711.

2. Joseph Addison (May 1, 1672—June 17, 1719) was an English essayist, poet, playwright, and politician. His name is usually remembered alongside that of his long-standing friend Richard Steele, with whom he founded *The Spectator* magazine. His simple prose style marked the end of the mannerisms and conventional classical images of the 17th century.

3. epitaph: An epitaph is a short piece of writing about someone who is dead, often carved on their gravestone.

4. depose: If a ruler or political leader is deposed, they are forced to give up their position.

5. When I see all these people whose identities, status, or positions are different are placed side by side after they die, it occurs to me that disputes or contradictions among people are so trivial.

Passage

Love Your Life[1]

Henry David Thoreau[2]

However mean your life is, meet it and live it; do not shun it and call it hard names[3]. It is not so bad as you are. It looks poorest when you're richest. The fault-finder will find faults even in paradise. Love your life, poor as it is. You may perhaps have some pleasant, thrilling, glorious hours, even in a poor-house. The setting sun is reflected from the windows of the alms-house as brightly as from the rich man's abode; the snow melts before its door as early in the spring. I do not see but a quiet mind may live as contentedly there, and have as cheering thoughts, as in a palace. The town's poor seem to me often to live the most independent lives of any. Maybe they are simply great enough to receive without misgiving. Most think that they are above being supported by the town; but it often happens that they are not above supporting themselves by dishonest means, which should be more disreputable[4]. Cultivate poverty like a garden herb[5], like sage. Do not trouble yourself much to get new things, whether clothes or friends. Turn the old; return to them. Things do not change; we change[6].

1. This passage is an extract from *Walden* published by Empire Books in 2012.

2. Henry David Thoreau (July 12, 1817—May 6, 1862) was an American naturalist, essayist, poet, and philosopher. As a leading transcendentalist, he is best known for his book *Walden*, a reflection upon simple living in natural surroundings, and his essay "Civil Disobedience", an argument for disobedience to an unjust state.

3. shun it: deliberately avoid or keep away from it; call it hard names: curse it.

4. Most people think they are virtuous to live by themselves, but actually in a bad way, which may be looked down upon because they are not respectable.

5. Garden herb refers to the common and negligible plants in the garden. But we should treat them carefully as with poverty.

6. Our attitude towards life may change with time, but keep loving our life.

Passage

Advice to Youth[1]

Mark Twain[2]

Always obey your parents, when they are present. This is the best policy in the long run, because if you don't, they will make you[3]. Most parents think they know better than you do, and you can generally make more by humoring that superstition than you can by acting on your own better judgment.

Be respectful to your superiors, if you have any, also to strangers, and sometimes to others. If a person offend you, and you are in doubt as to whether it was intentional or not, do not resort to extreme measures[4]; simply watch your chance and hit him with a brick. That will be sufficient. If you shall find that he had not intended any offense, come out frankly and confess yourself in the wrong when you struck him; acknowledge it like a man and say you didn't mean to. Yes, always avoid violence; in this age of charity and kindliness, the time has gone by for such things. Leave dynamite[5] to the low and unrefined.

Go to bed early, get up early—this is wise. Some authorities say get up with the sun; some say get up with one thing, others with another. But a lark[6] is really the best thing to get up with. It gives you a splendid reputation with everybody to know that you get up with the lark; and if you get the right kind of lark, and work at him right, you can easily train him to get up at half past nine, every time—it's no trick at all.

Notes

1. This passage is an extract from *Mark Twain Speaking* published by University of Iowa Press in 1976.

2. Samuel Langhorne Clemens (November 30, 1835—April 21, 1910), best known by his pen name Mark Twain, was an American writer, humorist, entrepreneur, publisher, and lecturer. He was praised as the "greatest humorist the United States has produced", and William Faulkner called him "the father of American literature".

3. they will make you: They will do everything to make you obey them.

4. resort to extreme measures: Take extreme reactions to take a revenge.

5. Dynamite is a type of explosive that contains nitroglycerin. It means violence should be left to those people who are low and vulgar.

6. lark: A lark is a small brown bird which makes a pleasant sound.

Passage 5

What I Have Lived for[1]

Bertrand Russell[2]

Three passions, simple but overwhelmingly strong, have governed my life: the longing for love, the search for knowledge, and unbearable pity for the suffering of mankind. These passions, like great winds, have blown me hither and thither, in a wayward course, over a deep ocean of anguish, reaching to the very verge of despair[3].

I have sought love, first, because it brings ecstasy—ecstasy so great that I would often have sacrificed all the rest of life for a few hours of this joy. I have sought it, next,

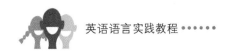

because it relieves loneliness—that terrible loneliness in which one shivering consciousness looks over the rim of the world into the cold unfathomable lifeless abyss[4]. I have sought it, finally, because in the union of love I have seen, in a mystic miniature, the prefiguring vision of the heaven that saints and poets have imagined. This is what I sought, and though it might seem too good for human life, this is what—at last—I have found.

With equal passion I have sought knowledge. I have wished to understand the hearts of men. I have wished to know why the stars shine. And I have tried to apprehend the Pythagorean[5] power by which number holds sway above the flux. A little of this, but not much, I have achieved.

Love and knowledge, so far as they were possible, led upward toward the heavens. But always pity brought me back to earth. Echoes of cries of pain reverberate in my heart. Children in famine, victims tortured by oppressors, helpless old people a burden to their sons, and the whole world of loneliness, poverty, and pain make a mockery of what human life should be. I long to alleviate the evil, but I cannot, and I too suffer.

Notes

1. This passage is an extract from *The Autobiography of Bertrand Russell* published by George Allen & Unwin in 1956.

2. Bertrand Arthur William Russell (May 18, 1872—February 2, 1970) was a Britishmathematician, philosopher, logician, and public intellectual. He had a considerable influence on mathematics, logic, set theory, linguistics, artificial intelligence, cognitive science, computer science and various areas of analytic philosophy, especially philosophy of mathematics, philosophy of language, epistemology, and metaphysics.

3. Simile is used here. These three passions have taken me from one place to another and brought me pain and desperation.

4. Unfathomable means that something cannot be understood or explained, usually because it is very strange or complicated. An abyss is a very deep hole in the ground. Unfathomable lifeless abyss describes a very hopeless and risky situation, which is brought by loneliness.

5. Pythagoras of Samos (c. 570 BC—c. 490 BC) was an ancient Ionian Greek philosopher, polymath and the eponymous founder of Pythagoreanism. His political and religious teachings were well known in Magna Graecia and influenced the philosophies of Plato, Aristotle, and, through them, the West in general. In antiquity, Pythagoras was credited with

many mathematical and scientific discoveries, including the Pythagorean theorem, Pythagorean tuning, the five regular solids, the Theory of Proportions, the sphericity of the Earth, and the identity of the morning and evening stars as the planet Venus.

Passage 6

Inaugural Address[1]

John Fitzgerald Kennedy[2]

To those old allies whose cultural and spiritual origins we share, we pledge the loyalty of faithful friends. United there is little we cannot do in a host of cooperative ventures. Divided there is little we can do—for we dare not meet a powerful challenge at odds and split asunder.[3]

To those new states whom we welcome to the ranks of the free, we pledge our word that one form of colonial control shall not have passed away merely to be replaced by a far more iron tyranny. We shall not always expect to find them supporting our view. But we shall always hope to find them strongly supporting their own freedom—and to remember that, in the past, those who foolishly sought power by riding the back of the tiger ended up inside[4].

To those people in the huts[5] and villages of half the globe struggling to break the bonds of mass misery, we pledge our best efforts to help them help themselves, for whatever period is required—not because the communists may be doing it, not because we seek their votes, but because it is right. If a free society cannot help the many who are poor, it cannot save the few who are rich.

Notes

1. This passage is an extract from John F. Kennedy's Inaugural Address in 1961.

2. John Fitzgerald Kennedy (May 29, 1917—November 22, 1963), often referred to by his initials JFK and by the nickname Jack, was an American politician who served as the 35th president of the United States from 1961 until his assassination in 1963. He was the youngest person to assume the presidency by election and the youngest president at the end of his tenure.

3. A comparison is made between "united" and "divided". "At odds" and "split

asunder" refer to the condition of disagreement and separation.

4. ended up inside: be swallowed by the tiger. It means people who sought power in a risky way will end up failing.

5. hut: A hut is a small house with only one or two rooms, especially one which is made of wood, mud, grass, or stones, referring to the poor condition.

Passage 7

Equality and Greatness[1]

George Bernard Shaw[2]

Between persons of equal income there is no social distinction except the distinction of merit. Money is nothing: character, conduct, and capacity are everything. Instead of all the workers being leveled down to low wage standards, and all the rich leveled up to fashionable income standards, everybody under a system of equal incomes would find her and his own natural level[3]. There would be great people and ordinary people and little people, but the great would always be those who had done great things, and never the idiots whose mothers had spoiled them and whose fathers had left them a hundred thousand a year; and the little would be persons of small minds and mean characters, and not poor persons who had never had a chance. That is why idiots are always in favour of inequality of income (their only chance of eminence[4]), and the really great in favour of equality.

1. This passage is an extract from *The Intelligent Woman's Guide to Socialism and Capitalism* published by Welcome Rain Publishers in 2016.

2. George Bernard Shaw (July 26, 1856—November 2, 1950) was an Irish playwright, critic, polemicist and political activist. His influence on Western theatre, culture and politics extended from the 1880s to his death and beyond. With a range incorporating both contemporary satire and historical allegory, Shaw became the leading dramatist of his generation, and in 1925 was awarded the Nobel Prize for Literature.

3. This sentence emphasizes the equality in the society through income level.

4. eminence: Eminence is the quality of being very well-known and highly respected.

On Meeting the Celebrated[1]

William Somerset Maugham[2]

I have always wondered at the passion many people have to meet the celebrated. The prestige you acquire by being able to tell your friends that you know famous men proves only that you are yourself of small account[3]. The celebrated develop a technique to deal with the person they come across. They show the world a mask, often an impressive one, but take care to conceal their real selves. They play the part that is expected from them, and with practice learn to play it very well, but you are stupid if you think that this public performance of theirs corresponds with the man within[4].

I have been attached, deeply attached, to a few people; but I have been interested in men in general not for their own sakes, but for the sake of my work. I have not, as Kant[5] enjoined, regarded each man as an end in himself, but as material that might be useful to me as a writer. I have been more concerned with the obscure[6] than with the famous. They are more often themselves. They have had no need to create a figure to protect themselves from the world or to impress it. Their idiosyncrasies[7] have had more chance to develop in the limited circle of their activity, and since they have never been in the public eye it has never occurred to them that they have anything to conceal. They display their oddities because it has never struck them that they are odd. And after all it is with the common run of men that we writers have to deal; kings, dictators, commercial magnates are from our point of view very unsatisfactory. To write about them is a venture that has often tempted writers, but the failure that has attended their efforts shows that such beings are too exceptional to form a proper ground for a work of art[8]. They cannot be made real. The ordinary is the writer's richer field. Its unexpectedness, its singularity, its infinite variety afford unending material. The great man is too often all of a piece; it is the little man that is a bundle of contradictory elements. He is inexhaustible. You never come to the end of the surprises he has in store for you. For my part I would much sooner spend a month on a desert island with a veterinary surgeon than with a prime minister.

1. This passage is an extract from *The Summing Up* published by Penguin Books in 1978.

2. William Somerset Maugham (January 25, 1874—December 16, 1965) was an English writer, known for his plays, novels and short stories. He became a medical student in London and qualified as a physician in 1897. He never practised medicine, and became a full-time writer. By 1908 he had four plays running at once in the West End of London. He wrote his 32nd and last play in 1933, after which he abandoned the theatre and concentrated on novels and short stories.

3. If a person, a country, or an organization has prestige, they are admired and respected because of the position they hold or the things they have achieved. People who need to show his or her own prestige through meeting celebrities only indicates that he or she is not a celebrity.

4. His public performance of theirs corresponds with the man within—the nature of him is not the same with the appearance of him.

5. Immanuel Kant (April 22, 1724—February 12, 1804) was a German philosopher and one of the central Enlightenment thinkers. Born in Königsberg, Kant's comprehensive and systematic works in epistemology, metaphysics, ethics, and aesthetics have made him one of the most influential figures in modern Western philosophy.

6. obscure: If something or someone is obscure, they are unknown, or are known by only a few people.

7. idiosyncrasies: If you talk about the idiosyncrasies of someone or something, you are referring to their rather unusual habits or characteristics.

8. Writer often want but fail to write about those beings because they are too special to be written about.

Passage 9

Immortality[1]

William Hazlitt[2]

As we grow old, our sense of the value of time becomes vivid. Nothing else, indeed, seems of any consequence. We can never cease wondering that that which has ever been should cease to be[3]. We find many things remain the same; why then should there be change in us. This adds a convulsive[4] grasp of whatever is, a sense of fallacious hollowness in all we see. Instead of the full pulpy feeling of youth tasting existence and every object in it, all is flat and vapid—a whited sepulchre[5], fair without but full of ravening and all uncleanness within. The world is a witch that puts us off with false shows and appearances. The simplicity of youth, the confiding expectation, the boundless raptures, are gone: we only think of getting out of it as well as we can, and without any great mischance or annoyance. The flush of illusion, even the complacent retrospect of past joys and hopes, is over: if we can slip out of life without indignity, and escape with little bodily infirmity, and frame our minds in the calm and respectable composure of still-life before we return to absolute nothingness, it is as much as we can expect. We do not die wholly at our deaths: we have mouldered away gradually long before[6]. Faculty after faculty, interest after interest, attachment after attachment disappear: we are torn from ourselves while living, year after year sees us no longer the same, and death only consigns the last fragment of what we were to the grave. That we should wear out by slow stages, and dwindle at last into nothing, is not wonderful, when even in our prime our strongest impressions leave little trace but for the moment and we are the creatures of petty circumstance. How little effect is made on us in our best days by the books we have read, the scenes we have witnessed, the sensations we have gone though!

Notes

1. This passage is an extract from "On the Feeling of Immortality in Youth" published by *The Monthly Magazine* in 1827.

2. William Hazlitt (April 10, 1778—September 18, 1830) was an English essayist, drama and literary critic, painter, social commentator, and philosopher. He is now considered one of the greatest critics and essayists in the history of the English language, placed in the company of Samuel Johnson and George Orwell. He is also acknowledged as the finest art critic of his age.

3. We are always wondering that what have existed should not exist any longer.

4. convulsive: A convulsive movement or action is sudden and cannot be controlled.

5. Whited sepulchre refers to one who is outwardly attractive, but unclean or vile on the inside; a hypocrite.

6. We do not die at once; we fade away gradually.

Passage 10

Lord Byron[1]

William Hazlitt

Intensity is the great and prominent distinction of Lord Byron's[2] writings. He seldom gets beyond force of style, nor has he produced any regular work or masterly whole. He does not prepare any plan beforehand, nor revise and retouch what he has written with polished accuracy. His only object seems to be to stimulate himself and his readers for the moment—to keep both alive, to drive away ennui[3], to substitute a feverish and irritable state of excitement for listless indolence or even calm enjoyment. For this purpose he pitches on any subject at random without much thought or delicacy. He is only impatient to begin, and takes care to adorn and enrich it as he proceeds with "thoughts that breathe and words that burn." He composes (as he himself has said) whether he is in the bath, in his study, or on horseback; he writes as habitually as others talk or think; and whether we have the inspiration of the Muse or not, we always find the spirit of the man of genius breathing from his verse. He grapples with his subject, and moves, penetrates, and animates it by the electric force of his own feelings. He is often monotonous, extravagant, offensive; but he is never dull, or tedious, but when he writes prose.

Lord Byron does not exhibit a new view of nature, or raise insignificant objects into importance by the romantic associations with which he surrounds them, but generally (at least) takes common-place thoughts and events, and endeavours to express them in stronger and statelier language than others. His poetry stands like a Martello tower[4] by the side of his subject. He does not, like Mr. Wordsworth[5], lift poetry from the ground, or create a sentiment out of nothing. He does not describe a daisy or a periwinkle, but the cedar or the cypress: not "poor men's cottages, but princes' palaces."

Notes

1. This passage is an extract from *The Spirit of the Age* published by Henry Colburn in 1825.

2. George Gordon Byron, (January 22, 1788—April 19, 1824) was an English romantic poet and peer. He was one of the leading figures of the Romantic movement, and

has been regarded as among the greatest of English poets. Among his best-known works are the lengthy narratives *Don Juan* and *Childe Harold's Pilgrimage*; many of his shorter lyrics in *Hebrew Melodies* also became popular.

3. ennui: Ennui is a feeling of being tired, bored, and dissatisfied.

4. Martello towers, sometimes known simply as Martellos, are small defensive forts that were built across the British Empire during the 19th century, from the time of the French Revolutionary Wars onwards. They stand up to 40 feet (12 m) high (with two floors) and typically had a garrison of one officer and 15—25 men.

5. William Wordsworth (April 7, 1770—April 23, 1850) was an English Romantic poet who, with Samuel Taylor Coleridge, helped to launch the Romantic Age in English literature with their joint publication *Lyrical Ballads* (1798).

Passage

Sonnet 18[1]

William Shakespeare[2]

Shall I compare thee[3] to a summer's day?
Thou[4] art[5] more lovely and more temperate:
Rough winds do shake the darling buds of May,
And summer's lease hath[6] all too short a date;
Sometime too hot the eye of heaven shines,
And often is his gold complexion dimmed,
And every fair from fair sometime declines,
By chance or nature's changing course untrimmed:[7]
But thy[8] eternal summer shall not fade,
Nor lose possession of that fair thou ow'st;
Nor shall Death brag thou wand'rest in his shade,
When in eternal lines to time thou grow'st.
So long as men can breathe or eyes can see,
So long lives this, and this gives life to thee.

Notes

1. This passage is an extract from *The Sonnets* published by *Cambridge University Press* in 1996.

2. William Shakespeare (April 26, 1564—April 23, 1616) was an English playwright, poet and actor. He is widely regarded as the greatest writer in the English language and the world's pre-eminent dramatist. He is often called England's national poet and the "Bard of Avon". His extant works, including collaborations, consist of some 39 plays, 154 sonnets, three long narrative poems, and a few other verses, some of uncertain authorship.

3. Thee is an old-fashioned, poetic, or religious word for "you" when you are talking to only one person. It is used as the object of a verb or preposition.

4. Thou is an old-fashioned, poetic, or religious word for "you" when you are talking to only one person. It is used as the subject of a verb.

5. Art is a singular form of the present tense (indicative mood) of "be".

6. Hath is an old-fashioned third person singular form of the verb "have".

7. Everything beautiful must eventually fade away and lose its charm, either by chance or by the natural flow of time.

8. Thy is an old-fashioned, poetic, or religious word for "your" when you are talking to one person.

9. ow'st 同 own；wand'rest 同 wander；grow'st 同 grow。古英语第二人称单数后加-st 或-est。

Passage 12

The Road Not Taken[1]

Robert Frost[2]

Two roads diverged in a yellow wood,
And sorry I could not travel both
And be one traveler, long I stood
And looked down one as far as I could
To where it bent in the undergrowth;

Then took the other, as just as fair[3],
And having perhaps the better claim,
Because it was grassy and wanted wear[4];
Though as for that the passing there
Had worn them really about the same,

And both that morning equally lay[5]
In leaves no step had trodden black.
Oh, I kept the first for another day!
Yet knowing how way leads on to way,
I doubted if I should ever come back.

I shall be telling this with a sigh
Somewhere ages and ages hence:
Two roads diverged in a wood, and I—
I took the one less traveled by,
And that has made all the difference.

1. This passage is an extract from *Mountain Interval* published by Henry Holt & Company in 1924.

2. Robert Lee Frost (March 26, 1874—January 29, 1963) was an American poet. His work was initially published in England before it was published in the United States. Known for his realistic depictions of rural life and his command of American colloquial speech, Frost frequently wrote about settings from rural life in New England in the early 20th century, using them to examine complex social and philosophical themes.

3. as just as fair: as beautiful as the first one.

4. wanted wear: had not worn off due to the walking of the travelers.

5. Both the roads lay in front of me almost in the same condition that morning.

Passage 13

Open a Path to Cooperation Across the Pacific[1]

Xi Jinping

The world is now at a stage of major development, transformation, and adjustment. All countries are interdependent and increasingly connected to each other, and humanity faces many common challenges. Although geographically distant, China and the Latin American and Caribbean[2] states are all developing countries pursuing the common dream of world peace, prosperity, and a better life for our peoples. The Chinese people will work with the peoples of Latin America and the Caribbean in making a greater contribution to the building of a global community of shared future.

When I proposed international cooperation on the Belt and Road Initiative[3] four years ago, China offered to work with all interested parties to build a new platform of global cooperation, to boost interconnectivity, and to add new drivers for common development. The initiative has received warm support from the international community, including many Latin American and Caribbean countries. In ancient times Chinese ancestors braved[4] the oceans and opened up the maritime Silk Road[5] between China and Latin America. Today, as we roll out the blueprint for the Belt and Road Initiative, we strive to forge a route for cooperation across the Pacific, in order to draw closer the two lands of abundance of China and Latin America, and open a new era of friendly relations.

Let us sail together towards a better tomorrow for China and Latin America, and a better future for humanity.

1. This passage is an extract from *Xi Jinping: The Governance of China* Ⅲ published by Foreign Languages Press in 2022.

2. The Caribbean is a subregion of the Americas that includes the Caribbean Sea and its islands, some of which are surrounded by the Caribbean Sea and some of which border both the Caribbean Sea and the North Atlantic Ocean; the nearby coastal areas on the mainland are often also included in the region. The region is southeast of the Gulf of Mexico and the North American mainland, east of Central America, and north of South America.

3. The Belt and Road Initiative (BRI, or B&R), known within China as the One Belt One Road, is a global infrastructure development strategy adopted by the Chinese government in 2013 to invest in more than 150 countries and international organizations. It is considered a centerpiece of the Chinese leader Xi Jinping's foreign policy. The BRI forms a central component of Xi's "Major Country Diplomacy" (大国外交) strategy, which calls for China to assume a greater leadership role for global affairs in accordance with its rising power and status. As of January 2023, 151 countries were listed as having signed up to the BRI.

4. brave: If you brave unpleasant or dangerous conditions, you deliberately expose yourself to them, usually in order to achieve something.

5. The Maritime Silk Road or Maritime Silk Route is the maritime section of the historic Silk Road that connected Southeast Asia, China, the Indian subcontinent, the Arabian peninsula, Somalia, Egypt and Europe. It began by the 2nd century BCE and flourished later on until the 15th century CE.

Passage 14

A Path of Cooperation, Health, Recovery and Growth[1]

Xi Jinping

The sudden onslaught of COVID-19 represents a grave threat to the health and lives of people around the world. It has taken a heavy toll[2] on the global economy, posing a tough economic and social challenge to many countries—developing countries in particular.

To contain the epidemic, countries affected have taken robust and effective measures based on their national conditions, and achieved encouraging results. While addressing the COVID-19 outbreak, many countries are also striving to revive the economy and get social development back on track.

China always puts the people and their lives front and center[3] and will do what it can to bring about an early global victory against COVID-19 and an early economic recovery worldwide.

The epidemic is a stark[4] reminder that the destinies of all nations are closely connected, and we humans rise and fall together. Be it in taming the virus or achieving economic recovery, we cannot succeed without solidarity[5], cooperation and multilateralism[6].

Greater connectivity, openness and inclusiveness are essential if we are to overcome global crises of this kind and achieve long-term development.

This is where Belt and Road international cooperation can make a difference.

China is committed to peaceful development and mutually beneficial cooperation. We stand ready to work with all partners to build The Belt and Road and make it a path of cooperation in addressing common challenges, a path of health for protecting people's health and safety, a path of economic recovery and social development, and a path of growth to achieve our full development potential.

Let us join hands to strengthen high-quality Belt and Road cooperation and build a global community of shared future.

1. This passage is an extract from *Xi Jinping*: *The Governance of China* Ⅳ published by Foreign Languages Press in 2022.

2. take a heavy toll: If something takes its/a toll, it causes suffering, deaths, or damage.

3. front and center: very easy to see or notice, or getting the most attention in a situation.

4. stark: complete or extreme.

5. solidarity: If a group of people show solidarity, they show support for each other or for another group, especially in political or international affairs.

6. Multilateralism, in the form of membership in international institutions, serves to bind powerful nations, discourage unilateralism, and gives small powers a voice and influence that they could not otherwise exercise. For a small power to influence a great power, the Lilliputian strategy of small countries banding together to collectively bind a larger one can be effective. Similarly, multilateralism may allow one great power to influence another great power. For a great power to seek control through bilateral ties could be costly; it may require bargaining and compromise with the other great power.

Passage 15

Work Together to Build the Silk Road Economic Belt and The 21st Century Maritime Silk Road[1]

Xi Jinping

Over 2,000 years ago, our ancestors, trekking across vast steppes and deserts[2], opened the transcontinental passage connecting Asia, Europe and Africa, known today as the Silk Road. Our ancestors, navigating rough seas, created sea routes linking the East with the West, namely, the maritime Silk Road. These ancient silk routes opened windows of friendly engagement among nations, adding a splendid chapter to the history of human progress. The thousand-year-old "gilt bronze silkworm[3]" displayed at China's Shaanxi History Museum and the Belitung shipwreck[4] discovered in Indonesia bear witness to this exciting period of history.

Spanning thousands of miles and years, the ancient silk routes embody the spirit of peace and cooperation, openness and inclusiveness, mutual learning and mutual benefit. The Silk Road spirit has become a great heritage of human civilization.

...

An ancient Chinese saying goes, "A long journey can be covered only by taking one step at a time[5]". Similarly, there is an Arab proverb which says that the Pyramid was built by piling one stone on another. In Europe, there is also the saying that "Rome wasn't built in a day." The Belt and Road Initiative is a great undertaking which requires dedicated efforts. Let us pursue this initiative step by step and deliver outcome one by one. By doing so, we will bring true benefit to both the world and all our people!

1. This passage is an extract from a speech by Xi Jinping at the Opening Ceremony of The Belt and Road Forum for International Cooperation in 2017.

2. It indicates that our ancestors had gone through a lot of difficulties before they opened the transcontinental passage.

3. A gilt bronze model of a silkworm in the Western Han dynasty (鎏金铜蚕).

4. The Belitung shipwreck (also called the Tang shipwreck or Batu Hitam shipwreck) is the wreck of an Arabian dhow which sank around 830 AD. The ship completed the

outward journey from Arabia to China, but sank on the return journey from China, approximately 1.6 kilometres off the coast of Belitung Island, Indonesia. It is unclear why the ship was south of the typical route when it sank.

5. A long journey can be covered only by taking one step at a time: 不积跬步无以至千里.

Passage 16

Working Together for a China-Central Asia Community with a Shared Future[1]

Xi Jinping

Transformations of the world unseen in a century are unfolding at a faster pace. Changes of the world, of our times, and of the historical trajectory are taking place in ways like never before. Central Asia, the center of the Eurasian continent[2], is at a crossroads connecting the East and West, the South and North.

The world needs a stable Central Asia. The sovereignty, security, independence and territorial integrity of Central Asian countries must be upheld; their people's choice of development paths must be respected; and their efforts for peace, harmony and tranquility must be supported.

The world needs a prosperous Central Asia. A dynamic and prospering Central Asia will help people in the region achieve their aspiration for a better life. It will also lend strong impetus to global economic recovery.[3]

The world needs a harmonious Central Asia. As a Central Asian saying goes, "Brotherhood is more precious than any treasure." Ethnic conflicts, religious strife, and cultural estrangement are not the defining feature of the region. Instead, solidarity, inclusiveness, and harmony are the pursuits of the Central Asian people. No one has the right to sow discord or stoke confrontation in the region, let alone seek selfish political interests.[4]

1. This passage is an extract from a speech by Xi Jinping at the China-Central Asia

Summit in 2023. China-Central Asia Summit (中国-中亚峰会) is a diplomatic summit held by the leaders of the People's Republic of China and the five Central Asian countries (Kazakhstan, Kyrgyzstan, Uzbekistan, Tajikistan, and Turkmenistan).

2. Eurasia is the combined continental landmass of Europe and Asia, with the term being a portmanteau of its two constituents. Located primarily in the Northern and Eastern Hemispheres, it is bordered by the Atlantic Ocean on the west, the Pacific Ocean to the east, the Arctic Ocean on the north, and by Africa, the Mediterranean Sea, the Pacific Ocean and the Indian Ocean to the south.

3. The prosperity of Central Asia will contribute to the economic development of the whole world.

4. All countries in Central Asia should not provoke disputes or conflicts with others or just focus on their own political interests. They should work together to promote the development in this area.

Passage 17

Why a Classic Is a Classic[1]

Arnold Bennett[2]

What causes the passionate few to make such a fuss about literature? There can be only one reply. They find a keen and lasting pleasure in literature. They enjoy literature as some men enjoy beer. The recurrence of this pleasure naturally keeps their interest in literature very much alive. They are forever making new researches, forever practicing on themselves. They learn to understand themselves. They learn to know what they want. Their taste becomes surer and surer as their experience lengthens. They do not enjoy today what will seem tedious to them tomorrow. When they find a book tedious[3], no amount of popular clatter will persuade them that it is pleasurable; and when they find it pleasurable no chill silence of the street crowds will affect their conviction[4] that the book is good and permanent. They have faith in themselves. What are the qualities in a book which give keen and lasting pleasure to the passionate few? This is a question so difficult that it has never yet been completely answered. You may talk lightly about truth, insight, knowledge, wisdom, humor, and beauty. But these comfortable words do not really carry you very far, for each of them has to be defined, especially the first and last. It is all very well for Keats[5] in his airy manner to assert that beauty is truth, truth beauty, and that that is all he knows or needs to know. I, for one, need to know a lot more. And I never shall know. Nobody, not even Hazlitt[6] nor Sainte-Beuve[7], has ever finally explained why he thought a book beautiful. I take the first fine lines that come to hand—

> The woods of Arcady[8] are dead,
> And over is their antique joy—

and I say that those lines are beautiful because they give me pleasure. But why? No answer! I only know that the passionate few will, broadly, agree with me in deriving this mysterious pleasure from these lines. I am only convinced that the liveliness of our pleasure in those and many other lines by the same author will ultimately cause the majority to believe, by faith, that W. B. Yeats[9] is a genius. The one reassuring aspect of the literary affair is that the passionate few are passionate about the same things. A continuance of interest does, in actual practice, lead ultimately to the same judgments. There is only the difference in width of interest. Some of the passionate few lack catholicity[10,] or, rather, the whole of their interest is confined to one narrow channel; they have none left over. These men help specially to vitalize the reputations of the narrower geniuses, such as Crashaw[11]. But their active predilections[12] never contradict the general verdict of the passionate few; rather they reënforce[13] it.

A classic is a work which gives pleasure to the minority which is intensely and permanently interested in literature. It lives on because the minority, eager to renew the sensation of pleasure, is eternally curious and is therefore engaged in an eternal process of rediscovery. A classic does not survive for any ethical reason. It does not survive because it conforms to certain canons, or because neglect would not kill it. It survives because it is a source of pleasure, and because the passionate few can no more neglect it than a bee can neglect a flower. The passionate few do not read "the right things" because they are right. That is to put the cart before the horse. "The right things" are the right things solely because the passionate few *like* reading them. Hence—and I now arrive at my point—the one primary essential to literary taste is a hot interest in literature. If you have that, all the rest will come. It matters nothing that at present you fail to find pleasure in certain classics. The driving impulse of your interest will force you to acquire experience, and experience will teach you the use of the means of pleasure. You do not know the secret ways of yourself: that is all. A continuance of interest must inevitably bring you to the keenest joys. But, of course, experience may be acquired judiciously or injudiciously, just as Putney[14] may be reached *via* Walham Green[15] or *via* St. Petersburg[16].

Part One Selected Essays

 Notes

1. This passage is an extract from "Why a Classic Is a Classic", *by Arnold Bennett*, from his *Literary Taste: How to Form It*, New York, George H. Doran Company.

2. Arnold Bennett, in full Enoch Arnold Bennett, (born May 27, 1867, Hanley, Staffordshire, England—died March 27, 1931, London), British novelist, playwright, critic, and essayist whose major works form an important link between the English novel and the mainstream of European realism.

3. tedious: so lacking in interest as to cause mental weariness; using or containing too many words.

4. conviction: an unshakable belief in something without need for proof or evidence.

5. Keats refers to John Keats (born October 31, 1795, London, England—died February 23, 1821, Rome, Papal States [Italy]), English Romantic lyric poet who devoted his short life to the perfection of a poetry marked by vivid imagery, great sensuous appeal, and an attempt to express a philosophy through classical legend.

6. Hazlitt refers to William Hazlitt, (born April 10, 1778, Maidstone, Kent, England—died Sept. 18, 1830, Soho, London), English writer best known for his humanistic essays.

7. Sainte Beuve refers to Charles Augustin Sainte-Beuve (born December 23, 1804, Boulogne, France—died October 13, 1869, Paris), French literary historian and critic.

8. Arcady: a mountainous region of ancient Greece in the central of Peloponnesus; traditionally represented in literature as a place of pastoral innocence and contentment.

9. W. B. Yeats refers to William Butler Yeats (born June 13, 1865, Sandymount, Dublin, Ireland—died January 28, 1939, Roquebrune-Cap-Martin, France), Irish poet, dramatist, and prose writer, one of the greatest English-language poets of the 20th century. He received the Nobel Prize for Literature in 1923.

10. catholicity: the beliefs and practices of a Catholic Church.

11. Crashaw refers to Richard Crashaw (born c. 1613, London, England—died August 21, 1649, Loreto, Papal States [Italy]), English poet known for religious verse of vibrant stylistic ornamentation and ardent faith.

12. predilection: a predisposition in favor of something; a strong liking.

13. Reënforce refers to reenforce.

14. Putney: a district of south London.

15. Walham Green: A largely disused name for the area around Fulham Broadway, which is now the commercial heart of Fulham.

16. St. Petersburg: formerly (1914—1924) Petrograd and (1924—1991) Leningrad, city and port, extreme northwestern Russia, is a major historical and cultural centre and an important port. It is the second largest city of Russia and one of the world's major cities.

Passage

Sunday before the War[1]

A. Clutton-Brock[2]

So it is always when the mind is troubled among happy things, and then one almost wishes they could share one's troubles and become more real with it. It seemed on that Sunday that a golden age had lasted till yesterday, and that the earth had still to learn the news of its ending. And this change had come, not by the will of God, not even by the will of man, but because some few men far away were afraid to be open and generous with each other. There was a power in their hands so great that it frightened them. There was a spring that they knew they must not touch, and, like mischievous[3] and nervous children, they had touched it at last, and now all the world was to suffer for their mischief.

So the next morning one saw a reservist[4] in his uniform saying goodbye to his wife and children at his cottage gate and then walking up the hill that leads out of the valley with a cheerful smile still on his face. There was the first open sign of trouble, a very little one, and he made the least of it; and, after all, this valley is very far from any possible war, and its harvest and its vintage[5] of perry[6] and cider[7] will surely be gathered in peace.

But what happiness can there be in that peace, or what security in the mind of man, when the madness of war is let loose in so many other valleys? Here there is a beauty inherited from the past, and added to the earth by man's will; but the men here are of the same nature and subject to the same madness as those who are gathering to fight on the frontiers. We are all men with the same power of making and destroying, with the same divine[8] foresight[9] mocked by the same animal blindness. We ourselves may not be in fault today, but it is human beings in no way different from us who are doing what we abhor[10] and they abhor even while they do it. There is a fate, coming from the beast in our own past, that the present man in us has not yet mastered, and for the moment that fate seems a malignity[11] in the nature of the universe that mocks us even in the beauty of these lonely hills. But it is not so, for we are not separate and indifferent like the beasts; and if one nation for the moment forgets our common humanity and its future, then another must take over that sacred[12] charge and guard it without hatred or fear until the madness is passed. May that be our task now, so that we may wage war only for the future peace of the world and with the lasting courage that needs no stimulant[13] of hate.

1. This passage is an extract from "Sunday before the War", written by Arthur Clutton-Brock, quoted from *Appreciations of English Essays*, which is published by Shanghai Foreign Language Education Press in 2010.

2. Arthur Clutton-Brock (1868—1924) is an essayist, critic and journalist.

3. mischievous: behaving in a way, or describing behaviour, that is slightly bad but is not intended to cause serious harm or damage.

4. reservist: a person who is trained as a soldier and is ready to fight in the army if needed.

5. vintage: a particular year or place in which a wine is made, or the wine itself.

6. perry: an alcoholic drink made from pears.

7. cider: an alcoholic drink made from apples.

8. divine: connected with a god, or like a god.

9. foresight: the ability to judge correctly what is going to happen in the future and plan your actions based on this knowledge.

10. abhor: to hate sth., for example a way of behaving or thinking, especially for moral reasons.

11. malignity: intense ill will or hatred; great malice.

12. sacred: connected with God or a god; considered to be holy.

13. stimulant: something that makes or causes something else to grow or develop.

Passage 19

Affection[1]

Bertrand Russell[2]

The best type of affection is reciprocally[3] life-giving; each receives affection with joy and gives it without effort, and each finds the whole world more interesting in consequence of the existence of this reciprocal happiness. There is, however, another kind, by no means uncommon, in which one person sucks the vitality of the other, one receives what the other gives, but gives almost nothing in return. Some very vital people belong to this bloodsucking[4] type. They extract[5] the vitality from one victim after another, but while they prosper and grow interesting, those upon whom they live grow pale and dim and dull. Such people use others as means to their own ends, and never consider them as ends in themselves. Fundamentally they are not interested in those whom for the moment they think they love; they are interested only in the stimulus[6] to their own activities, perhaps of a quite impersonal sort. Evidently this springs from some defect in their nature, but it is one not altogether easy either to diagnose or to cure. It is a characteristic frequently associated with great ambition, and is rooted, I should say, in an unduly[7] one-sided view of what makes human happiness. Affection in the sense of a genuine reciprocal interest of two persons in each other, not solely as means to each other's good, is one of the most important elements of real happiness, and the man whose ego is so enclosed within steel walls that this enlargement of it is impossible misses the best that life has to offer, however successful he may be in his career. A too powerful ego[8] is a prison from which a man must escape if he is to enjoy the world to the full. A capacity for genuine affection is one of the marks of the man who has escaped from this prison of self. To receive affection is by no means enough; affection which is received should liberate the affection which is to be given, and only where both exist in equal measure does affection achieve its best possibilities.

Notes

1. This passage is an extract from Chapter 12 Affection in *The Conquest of Happiness*, published by Unwin Brothers Ltd.

2. Bertrand Russell (1872—1970), in full Bertrand Arthur William Russell, 3rd Earl Russell of Kingston Russell, Viscount Amberley of Amberley and of Ardsalla, British philosopher, logician, and social reformer, founding figure in the analytic movement in Anglo-American philosophy, and recipient of the Nobel Prize for Literature in 1950.

3. reciprocally: in a mutual or shared manner.

4. bloodsucking: of plants or persons, having the nature or habits of a parasite or leech, living off another.

5. extract: remove, usually with some force or effort; also used in an abstract sense.

6. stimulus: any stimulating information or event; acts to arouse action.
7. unduly: to an undue degree.
8. ego: an inflated feeling of pride in your superiority to others.

Passage

Companionship of Books[1]

Samual Smiles[2]

A man may usually be known by the books he reads as well as by the company he keeps; for there is a companionship of books as well as of men; and one should always live in the best company, whether it be of books or of men.

A good book may be among the best of friends. It is the same today that it always was, and it will never change. It is the most patient and cheerful of companions. It does not turn its back upon us in times of adversity[3] or distress. It always receives us with the same kindness, amusing and instructing us in youth, and comforting and consoling us in age.

Men often discover their affinity[4] to each other by the mutual[5] love they have for a book—just as two persons sometimes discover a friend by the admiration which both entertain for a third. There is an old proverb, "Love me, love my dog." But there is more wisdom in this: "Love me, love my book." The book is a truer and higher bond of union. Men can think, feel, and sympathize[6] with each other through their favorite author. They live in him together, and he in them.

"Books," said Hazlitt[7], "wind into the heart; the poet's verse slides into the current of our blood. We read them when young, we remember them when old. We read there of what has happened to others; we feel that it has happened to ourselves. They are to be had everywhere cheap and good. We breathe but the air of books. We owe everything to their authors, on this side barbarism."

A good book is often the best urn of a life, enshrining[8] the best thoughts of which that life was capable; for the world of a man's life is, for the most part, but the world of his thoughts. Thus the best books are treasuries of good words and golden thoughts, which, remembered and cherished, become our abiding companions and comforters. "They are never alone," said Sir Philip Sidney[9], "that are accompanied by noble thoughts." The good and true thought may in times of temptation be as an angel of mercy purifying and guarding the soul. It also enshrines the germs of action, for good words almost always inspire to good works.

...

Books possess an essence of immortality[10]. They are by far the most lasting products of human effort. Temples crumble into ruin; pictures and statues decay; but books survive. Time is of no account with great thoughts, which are as fresh today as when they first passed through their author's minds ages ago. What was then said and thought still speaks to us as vividly as ever from the printed page. The only effect of time has been to sift and winnow out the bad products; for nothing in literature can long survive but what is really good.

Notes

1. This passage is from a chapter of *Character*, written by Samuel Smiles, published originally in 1871 by John Murray.

2. Samuel Smiles (1812—1904), Scottish author best known for his didactic work *Self-Help* (1859), which, with its successors, *Character* (1871), *Thrift* (1875), and *Duty* (1880), enshrined the basic Victorian values associated with the "gospel of work".

3. adversity: a state of misfortune or affliction.

4. affinity: the attraction between an antigen and an antibody.

5. mutual: common to or shared by two or more parties.

6. sympathize: share the feelings of; understand the sentiments of.

7. Hazlitt refers to William Hazlitt (1778—1830), English writer best known for his humanistic essays.

8. enshrine: enclose in a shrine.

9. Sir Philip Sidney (1554—1586), Elizabethan courtier, statesman, soldier, poet, and patron of scholars and poets, considered the ideal gentleman of his day. After Shakespeare's sonnets, Sidney's *Astrophel and Stella* is considered the finest Elizabethan sonnet cycle.

10. immortality: the quality or state of being immortal.

Passage 21

Letter to Lord Chesterfield[1]

Samuel Johnson [2]

My Lord,

I have been lately informed by the proprietor[3] of *The World* that two papers in which my Dictionary is recommended to the public, were written by your Lordship. To be so distinguished is an honor which, being very little accustomed to favors from the Great, I know not well how to receive, or in what terms to acknowledge.

When upon some slight encouragement I first visited your Lordship I was overpowered[4] like the rest of mankind by the enchantment[5] of your address, and could not forbear[6] to wish that I might boast myself *le vainqueur du vainqueur de la terre*[7], that I might obtain that regard for which I saw the world contending, but I found my attendance so little encouraged, that neither pride nor modesty would suffer me to continue it. When I had once addressed your Lordship in public, I had exhausted all the art of pleasing which a retired and uncourtly[8] scholar can possess. I had done all that I could, and no man is well pleased to have his all neglected, be it ever so little.

Seven years, my Lord, have now passed, since I waited in your outward rooms, or was repulsed[9] from your door, during which time I have been pushing on my work through difficulties of which it is useless to complain, and have brought it at last to the verge of publication without one act of assistance, one word of encouragement, or one smile of favor. Such treatment I did not expect, for I never had a patron[10] before.

The shepherd[11] in Virgil grew at last acquainted with love, and found him a native of the rocks.

Is not a patron, my Lord, one who looks with unconcern on a man struggling for life in the water and when he has reached ground encumbers him with help? The notice which you have been pleased to take of my labours, had it been early, had been kind; but it has been delayed till I am indifferent and cannot enjoy it, till I am solitary[12] and cannot impart it, till I am known and do not want it.

I hope it is no very cynical[13] asperity[14] not to confess obligations where no benefit has been received, or to be unwilling that the public should consider me as owing that to a patron, which Providence has enabled me to do for myself.

Having carried on my work thus far with so little obligation to any favourer of learning I shall not be disappointed though I should conclude it, if less be possible, with less; for I have been long wakened from that dream of hope, in which I once boasted myself with so much exultation[15],

My Lord,
Your Lordship's most humble,
most obedient servant,
S. J

1. This is the famous letter from Samuel Johnson to the fourth Earl of Chesterfield on the subject of the Dictionary (1755)—the complex and ambitious work which took Johnson over eight years to complete. In the letter, Johnson vents his fury towards his supposed patron for neglecting him for seven years and then making a show of support when the Dictionary was nearly finished. With biting humour, Johnson asks, "Is not a patron, my Lord, one who looks with unconcern on a man struggling for life in the water and when he has reached ground encumbers him with help?"

2. Samuel Johnson (1709—1784), byname Dr. Johnson, is an English critic, biographer, essayist, poet, and lexicographer, regarded as one of the greatest figures of 18th-century life and letters.

3. proprietor: someone who owns (is legal possessor of) a business.

4. overpowered: overcome by superior force.

5. enchantment: a feeling of great liking for something wonderful and unusual.

6. forbear: refrain from doing; resist doing something.

7. le vainqueur du vainqueur de la terre: the winner of the earth.

8. uncourtly: not related to.

9. repulsed: cause to move back by force or influence.

10. patron: someone who supports or champions something.

11. shepherd: a herder of sheep (on an open range); someone who keeps the sheep together in a flock.

12. solitary: confinement of a prisoner in isolation from other prisoner.

13. cynical: believing the worst of human nature and motives; having a sneering disbelief in e. g. selflessness of others.

14. asperity: something hard to endure.

15. exultation: a feeling of extreme joy.

Passage 22

Of Studies[1]

Francis Bacon[2]

Studies serve for delight, for ornament[3], and for ability. Their chief use for delight, is in privateness and retiring; for ornament, is in discourse; and for ability, is in the judgment and disposition of business. For expert and execute, and perhaps judge of particulars, one by one; but the general counsels, and the plots and marshalling[4] of affairs come best form those that are learned. To spend too much time in studies is sloth; to use them too much for ornament, is affectation; to make judgement wholly by their rules, is the humour of a scholar. They perfect nature, and are perfected by experience, for natural abilities are like natural plants, that need pruning by study; and studies themselves do give forth directions too much at large, except they be bounded in by experience. Crafty men contemn studies, simple men admire them, and wise men use them; for they teach not their own use; but that is a wisdom without them and above them, won by observation. Read not to contradict and confute[5]; nor to believe and take for granted; nor to find talk and discourse; but to weigh and consider. Some books are to be tasted, others to be swallowed, and some few to be chewed and digested; that is, some books are to be read only in parts; others to be read, but not curiously; and some few to be read wholly, and with diligence and attention. Some books also may be read by deputy, and extracts made of them by others; but that would be only in the less important arguments, and the meaner sort of books; else distilled books are like common distilled waters, flashy things. Reading maketh a full man; conference a ready man; and writing an exact man. And therefore, if a man write little, he had need have a great memory; if he confer little, he had need have a present wit; and if he read little, he had need have much cunning[6,] to seem to know that he doth not. Histories make men wise, poets witty, the mathematics subtile[7], natural philosophy deep, moral grave, logic and rhetoric able to contend. *Abeunt studia in mores.*

1. This is an essay from *The Essays of Francis Bacon*, written by Francis Bacon, published by Beijing Foreign Language Teaching and Research Press in 2020.

2. Francis Bacon (1561—1626), in full Francis Bacon, Viscount Saint Alban, also called (1603—1618) Sir Francis Bacon, lord chancellor of England (1618—1621), is a lawyer, statesman, philosopher, and master of the English tongue.

3. ornament: something used to beautify.

4. marshal: a law officer having duties similar to those of a sheriff in carrying out the judgments of a court of law.

5. cunning: shrewdness as demonstrated by being skilled in deception.

Passage 23

Gettysburg Address[1]

Abraham Lincoln[2]

Four score and seven years ago our fathers brought forth on this continent, a new nation, conceived in Liberty, and dedicated to the proposition that all men are created equal.

Now we are engaged in a great civil war, testing whether that nation, or any nation so conceived and so dedicated, can long endure. We are met on a great battlefield of that war. We have come to dedicate a portion of that field, as a final resting place for those who here gave their lives that that nation might live. It is altogether fitting and proper that we should do this.

But, in a larger sense, we cannot dedicate—we cannot consecrate[3]—we cannot hallow[4]—this ground. The brave men, living and dead, who struggled here, have consecrated it, far above our poor power to add or detract[5]. The world will little note, nor long remember what we say here, but it can never forget what they did here. It is for us the living, rather, to be dedicated here to the unfinished work which they who fought here have thus far so nobly advanced. It is rather for us to be here dedicated to the great task remaining before us—that from these honored dead we take increased devotion to that cause for which they gave the last full measure of devotion—that we here highly resolve that these dead shall not have died in vain—that this nation, under God, shall have a new birth of freedom—and that government of the people, by the people, for the people, shall not perish[6] from the earth.

Part One Selected Essays

1. Gettysburg Address, world-famous speech delivered by U. S. President Abraham Lincoln at the dedication (November 19, 1863) of the National Cemetery at Gettysburg, Pennsylvania, the site of one of the decisive battles of the American Civil War (July 1—3, 1863).

2. Abraham Lincoln (1809—1865), byname Honest Abe, the Rail-Splitter, or the Great Emancipator, 16th president of the United States (1861—1865), who preserved the Union during the American Civil War and brought about the emancipation of enslaved people in the United States.

3. consecrate: solemnly dedicated to or set apart for a high purpose.

4. hallow: render holy by means of religious rites.

5. detract: take away a part from; diminish.

6. perish: pass from physical life and lose all bodily attributes and functions necessary to sustain life.

Passage 24

First Snow[1]

John Boynton Priestley[2]

When I got up this morning, the world was a chilled hollow of dead white and faint blues. The light that came through the windows was very queer, and it contrived[3] to make the familiar business of splashing and shaving and brushing and dressing very queer too. Then the sun came out, and by the time I had sat down to breakfast, it was shining bravely and flushing the snow with delicate pinks. The dining-room window had been transformed into a lovely Japanese print. The little plum-tree outside, with the faintly flushed snow lining its boughs[4] and artfully disposed along its trunk, stood in full sunlight. An hour or two later, everything was a cold glitter of white and blue. The world had completely changed again. The little Japanese prints had all vanished. I looked out of my study window, over the garden, the meadow, to the low hills beyond, and the ground was one long glare, the sky was steely[5], and all the trees so many black and sinister[6] shapes. There was indeed something curiously sinister about the whole prospect. It was as if our kindly countryside, closed to the very heart of England, had been turned into a cruel steppe[7]. At any moment, it seemed, a body of horsemen might be seen breaking out from the black copse, so many instruments of tyranny[8], and shots might be heard and some distant patch of snow be reddened. It was that kind of landscape.

Now it has changed again. The glare has gone and no touch of the sinister remains. But the snow is falling heavily, in great soft flakes, so that you can hardly see across the shallow valley, and the roofs are thick and the trees all bending, and the weathercock of the village church, still to be seen through the grey loaded air, has become some creature out of Hans Andersen[9]. From my study, which is apart from the house and faces it, I can see the children flattening their noses against the nursery window, and there is running through my head a jangle of rhyme I used to repeat when I was a child and flattened my nose against the cold window to watch the falling snow:

Snow, snow faster:

White alabaster[10]!

Killing geese in Scotland,

Sending feathers here!

Notes

1. This passage is an extract from *Apes and Angels*, *which is published in* 1928.

2. J. B. Priestley (1894—1984), British novelist, playwright, and essayist, noted for his varied output and his ability for shrewd characterization.

3. contrived: showing effects of planning or manipulation.

4. bough: any of the larger branches of a tree.

5. steely: resembling steel as in hardness.

6. sinister: threatening or foreshadowing evil or tragic developments.

7. steppe: extensive plain without trees (associated with eastern Russia and Siberia).

8. tyranny: a form of government in which the ruler is an absolute dictator (not restricted by a constitution or laws or opposition etc.)

9. Hans Andersen (1805—1875), Danish master of the literary fairy tale whose stories achieved wide renown. He is also the author of plays, novels, poems, travel books, and several autobiographies.

10. alabaster: a compact fine-textured, usually white gypsum used for carving.

How to Grow Old[1]

Bertrand Russell[2]

Psychologically there are two dangers to be guarded against in old age. One of these is undue absorption[1] in the past. It does not do to live in memories, in regrets for the good old days, or in sadness about friends who are dead. One's thoughts must be directed to the future, and to things about which there is something to be done. This is not always easy; one's own past is a gradually increasing weight. It is easy to think to oneself that one's emotions used to be more vivid than they are, and one's mind more keen. If this is true it should be forgotten, and if it is forgotten it will probably not be true.

The other thing to be avoided is clinging to youth in the hope of sucking vigor from its vitality. When your children are grown up they want to live their own lives, and if you continue to be as interested in them as you were when they were young, you are likely to become a burden to them, unless they are unusually callous[4]. I do not mean that one should be without interest in them, but one's interest should be contemplative[5] and, if possible, philanthropic[6], but not unduly emotional. Animals become indifferent to their young as soon as their young can look after themselves, but human beings, owing to the length of infancy, find this difficult.

I think that a successful old age is easiest for those who have strong impersonal interests involving appropriate activities. It is in this sphere that long experience is really fruitful, and it is in this sphere that the wisdom born of experience can be exercised without being oppressive. It is no use telling grown-up children not to make mistakes, both because they will not believe you, and because mistakes are an essential part of education. But if you are one of those who are incapable of impersonal interests, you may find that your life will be empty unless you concern yourself with your children and grandchildren. In that case you must realize that while you can still render them material services, such as making them an allowance or knitting them jumpers, you must not expect that they will enjoy your company.

1. This passage is an extract from *Portraits from Memory and Other Essays*, written by

Bertrand Russell, published in 1951 by Simon and Schuster in New York.

2. Bertrand Russell (1872—1970) is a British philosopher, logician, and social reformer, founding figure in the analytic movement in Anglo-American philosophy, and recipient of the Nobel Prize for Literature in 1950.

3. absorption: complete attention; intense mental effort.

4. callous: emotionally hardened.

5. contemplative: a person devoted to the contemplative life.

6. philanthropic: generous in assistance to the poor.

Passage 26

Solitude[1]

Henry David Thoreau[2]

I find it wholesome to be alone the greater part of the time. To be in company, even with the best, is soon wearisome[3] and dissipating[4]. I love to be alone. I never found the companion that was so companionable as solitude. We are for the most part more lonely when we go abroad among men than when we stay in our chambers. A man thinking or working is always alone, let him be where he will. Solitude is not measured by the miles of space that intervene between a man and his fellows. The really diligent student in one of the crowded hives of Cambridge College is as solitary as a dervish[5] in the desert. The farmer can work alone in the field or the woods all day, hoeing[6] or chopping, and not feel lonesome, because he is employed; but when he comes home at night he cannot sit down in a room alone, at the mercy of his thoughts, but must be where he can "see the folks," and recreate, and as he thinks remunerate[7] himself for his day's solitude; and hence he wonders how the student can sit alone in the house all night and most of the day without ennui and "the blues;" but he does not realize that the student, though in the house, is still at work in *his* field, and chopping in *his* woods, as the farmer in his, and in turn seeks the same recreation and society that the latter does, though it may be a more condensed form of it.

Society is commonly too cheap. We meet at very short intervals, not having had time to acquire any new value for each other. We meet at meals three times a day, and give each other a new taste of that old musty[8] cheese that we are. We have had to agree on a certain set of rules, called etiquette and politeness, to make this frequent meeting tolerable, and that we need not come to open war. We meet at the post-office, and at the sociable, and about the fireside every night; we live thick and are in each other's way, and stumble over one another, and I think that we thus lose some respect for one another. Certainly less frequency would suffice for all important and hearty communications. Consider the girls in a factory,—never alone, hardly in their dreams. It would be better if there were but one inhabitant to a square mile, as where I live. The value of a man is not in his skin, that we should touch him.

I have heard of a man lost in the woods and dying of famine and exhaustion at the foot of a tree, whose loneliness was relieved by the grotesque[9] visions with which, owing to bodily weakness, his diseased imagination surrounded him, and which he believed to be real. So also, owing to bodily and mental health and strength, we may be continually cheered by a like but more normal and natural society, and come to know that we are never alone.

1. This passage is an extract from *Walden*, written by Henry David Thoreau, published by Houghton Mifflin Company in 1964. In an age of growing complexity, Thoreau's call for simplicity, sounded more than one hundred years ago from the shores of Walden Pond, rings with ever-mounting insistence. *Walden* is a national classic not merely because it has endured but because it refuses to be ignored.

2. Henry David Thoreau (1817—1862), American essayist, poet, and practical philosopher renowned for having lived the doctrines of Transcendentalism as recorded in his masterwork, *Walden* (1854).

3. wearisome: so lacking in interest as to cause mental weariness.

4. dissipating: break up and scatter.

5. dervish: an ascetic Muslim monk; a member of an order noted for devotional exercises involving bodily movements.

6. hoeing: dig with a hoe.

7. remunerate: make payment to; compensate.

8. musty: covered with or smelling of mold.

9. grotesque: distorted and unnatural in shape or size; abnormal and hideous.

A Liberal Education[1]

T. H. Huxley[2]

By way of a beginning, let us ask ourselves—What is education? Above all things, what is our ideal of a thoroughly liberal education? —of that education which, if we could begin life again, we would give ourselves—of that education which, if we could mould the fates to our own will, we would give our children? Well, I know not what may be your conceptions upon this matter, but I will tell you mine, and I hope I shall find that our views are not very discrepant[3].

Suppose it were perfectly certain that the life and fortune of every one of us would, one day or other, depend upon his winning or losing a game at chess. Don't you think that we should all consider it to be a primary duty to learn at least the names and the moves of the pieces; to have a notion of a gambit[4], and a keen eye for all the means of giving and getting out of check? Do you not think that we should look with a disapprobation[5] amounting to scorn, upon the father who allowed his son, or the state which allowed its members, to grow up without knowing a pawn from a knight?

Yet, it is a very plain and elementary truth that the life, the fortune, and the happiness of every one of us, and, more or less, of those who are connected with us, do depend upon our knowing something of the rules of a game infinitely more difficult and complicated than chess. It is a game which has been played for untold ages, every man and woman of us being one of the two players in a game of his or her own. The chessboard is the world, the pieces are the phenomena of the universe, the rules of the game are what we call the laws of Nature. The player on the other side is hidden from us. We know that his play is always fair, just and patient. But also we know, to our cost, that he never overlooks a mistake, or makes the smallest allowance for ignorance. To the man who plays well, the highest stakes are paid, with that sort of overflowing generosity with which the strong shows delight in strength. And one who plays ill is checkmated[6]—without haste, but without remorse[7].

My metaphor will remind some of you of the famous picture in which Retzsch has depicted Satan playing at chess with man for his soul. Substitute for the mocking fiend in that picture a calm, strong angel who is playing for love, as we say, and would rather lose than win—and I should accept it as an image of human life.

Well, what I mean by Education is learning the rules of this mighty game. In other words, education is the instruction of the intellect in the laws of Nature, under which name I include not merely things and their forces, but men and their ways; and the fashioning of the affections and of the will into an earnest and loving desire to move in harmony with those laws. For me, education means neither more nor less than this. Anything which professes to call itself education must be tried by this standard, and if it fails to stand the test, I will not call it education, whatever may be the force of authority or of numbers upon the other side.

Notes

1. This passage is an extract from "A Liberal Education", written by Thomas Henry Huxley, reprinted in Roger Sherman Loomis's Freshman Readings, Boston, Houghton Mifflin Company, 1925.

2. Thomas Henry Huxley (1825—1895), English biologist, educator, and advocate of agnosticism (he coined the word). Huxley's vigorous public support of Charles Darwin's evolutionary naturalism earned him the nickname "Darwin's bulldog," while his organizational efforts, public lectures, and writing helped elevate the place of science in modern society.

3. discrepant: not compatible with other facts.

4. gambit: an opening remark intended to secure an advantage for the speaker.

5. disapprobation: an expression of strong disapproval; pronouncing as wrong or morally culpable.

6. checkmated: complete victory.

7. remorse: a feeling of deep regret (usually for some misdeed).

Passage 28

An Afternoon Walk in October[1]

William Hale White[2]

It was a day by itself, coming after a fortnight's storm and rain. The sun did not shine clearly, but it spread through the clouds a tender, diffused[3] light, crossed by level cloud-bars, which stretched to a great length, quite parallel. The tints[4] in the sky were wonderful, every conceivable shade of blue-grey, which contrived to modulate[5] into the golden brilliance in which the sun was veiled. I went out in the afternoon. It was too early in the year for a heavy fall of leaves, but nevertheless the garden was covered. They were washed to the sides of the roads, and lay heaped up over the road-gratings, masses of gorgeous harmonies in red, brown, and yellow. The chestnuts and acorns[6] dropped in showers, and the patter on the gravel was a little weird. The chestnut husks split wide open when they came to the ground, revealing the polished brown of the shy fruit.

The lavish[7], drenching[8], downpour in extravagant[9] excess had been glorious. I went down to the bridge to look at the floods. The valley was a great lake, reaching to the big trees in the fields which had not yet lost the fire in their branches. The river-channel could be discerned only by the boiling of the current. It has risen above the crown of the main stone arch[10], and swirled[11] and plunged underneath it. A furious backwater, repulsed from the smaller arch, aided the tumult[12]. The wind had gone and there was perfect silence, save for the agitation of the stream, but a few steps upwards the gentle tinkle of the little runnels could be beard in their deeply-cut, dark, and narrow channels. In a few minutes they were caught up, rejoicing, in the embrace of the deep river which would carry them with it to the sea. They were safe now from being lost in the earth.

I went a little further up the hill: a flock of about fifty sheep were crossing from a field on one side of the road to another directly opposite. They were packed close together, and their backs were an undulating[13] continuous surface. The shepherd was pursuing a stray sheep, and they stood still for a minute in the middle of the road. A farmer came up in his gig and was held back. He used impatient language. O farmer! which is of more importance to the heavenly powers—that you should not be stopped, or that the sheep should loiter[14] and go into that field at their own pace? All sheep, by the way, look sad. Perhaps they are dimly aware of their destiny.

Notes

1. This passage is an extract from *Last Pages from a Journal: With Other Papers*, written by Mark Rutherford (William Hale White), published by Oxford University Press in 1915.

2. William Hale White (1831—1913), with pseudonym Mark Rutherford, English novelist noted for his studies of Nonconformist experience.

3. diffused: (of light rays) subjected to scattering by reflection from a rough surface or transmission through a translucent material.

4. tint: a quality of a given color that differs slightly from another color.
5. modulate: change the key of, in music.
6. acorn: fruit of the oak tree; a smooth thin-walled nut in a woody cup-shaped base.
7. lavish: very generous.
8. drenching: the act of making something completely wet.
9. extravagant: unrestrained, especially with regard to feelings.
10. arch: a curved shape in the vertical plane that spans an opening.
11. swirled: the shape of something rotating rapidly.
12. tumult: a state of commotion and noise and confusion.
13. undulating: stir up (water) so as to form ripples.
14. loiter: be about.

Passage 29

Insouciance[1]

D. H. Lawrence[2]

My balcony[3] is on the east side of the hotel, and my neighbours on the right are a Frenchman, white-haired, and his white-haired wife; my neighbours on the left are two little white-haired English ladies. And we are all mortally[4] shy of one another.

When I peep out of my room in the morning and see the matronly[5] French lady in a purple silk wrapper, standing like the captain on the bridge surveying the morning, I pop in again before she can see me. And whenever I emerge during the day, I am aware of the two little white-haired ladies popping back like two white rabbits, so that literally I only see the whisk[6] of their skirt-hems.

This afternoon being hot and thundery, I woke up suddenly and went out on the balcony barefoot. There I sat serenely[7] contemplating the world, and ignoring the two bundles of feet of the two little ladies which protruded[8] from their open doorways, upon the end of the two *chaises longues*. A hot, still afternoon! The lake shining rather glassy away below, the mountains rather sulky, the greenness very green, all a little silent and lurid, and two mowers mowing with scythes[9], downhill just near: *slush! slush!* sound the scythe-strokes.

The two little ladies become aware of my presence. I become aware of a certain agitation[10] in the two bundles of feet wrapped in two discreet steamer rugs and protruding on the end of two *chaises longues* from the pair of doorways upon the balcony next me. One bundle of feet suddenly disappears; so does the other. Silence!

Then lo! with odd sliding suddenness a little white-haired lady in grey silk, with round blue eyes, emerges and looks straight at me, and remarks that it is pleasant now. A little cooler, say I, with false amiability[11]. She quite agrees, and we speak of the men mowing; how plainly one hears the long breaths of the scythes!

By now we are *tête-à-tête*[12]. We speak of cherries, strawberries, and the promise of the vine crop. This somehow leads to Italy, and to Signor Mussolini[13]. Before I know where I am, the little white-haired lady has swept me off my balcony, away from the glassy lake, the veiled mountains, the two men mowing, and the cherry trees, away into the troubled ether of international politics.

Notes

1. This passage is an extract from *Assorted Articles*, written by D. H. Lawrence, published by Martin Secker in 1930.

2. D. H. Lawrence (1885—1930), in full David Herbert Lawrence, English author of novels, short stories, poems, plays, essays, travel books, and letters. His novels *Sons and Lovers* (1913), *The Rainbow* (1915), and *Women in Love* (1920) made him one of the most influential English writers of the 20th century.

3. balcony: a platform projecting from the wall of a building and surrounded by a balustrade or railing or parapet.

4. mortally: in such a manner that death ensues (also in reference to hatred, jealousy, fear, etc.).

5. matronly: befitting or characteristic of a fully mature woman.

6. whisk: a mixer incorporating a coil of wires; used for whipping eggs or cream.

7. serenely: in a peacefully serene manner.

8. protruded: extend out or project in space.

9. scythe: an edge tool for cutting grass; has a long handle that must be held with both hands and a curved blade that moves parallel to the ground.

10. agitation: a mental state of extreme emotional disturbance.

11. amiability: a cheerful and agreeable mood.

12. tête-à-tête: a private conversation between two people.

Part One Selected Essays

Passage 30

Our Party's Mission Is to Serve the People[1]

Xi Jinping

Our Party's mission is to serve the people and to improve their lives.

Your village is in the Lüliang Mountains, near the Yellow River, and across the river is Shaanxi Province. In the late 1960s, I was sent to work as a farmer in Shaanxi's Yanchuan County, which is not far from here. Its hilly terrain[2] and ravines are similar to the landscape here. The Loess Plateau[3] is our home, and the home of our ancestors. It has nurtured our Chinese civilization.

In the past, people of my age led a hard life. Even those living in cities wore patched clothes. I used to spin and weave during my farming years. In the past, I was always dismayed and concerned to see how hard life was for some people. But now, our rural areas have changed significantly. Food, clothing, and consumer goods have all improved, and the lack of basic necessities that troubled the Chinese for several thousand years has been addressed once and for all.

During this trip to Shanxi, I have been to two villages. I am delighted to see that you now lead a life of contentment. Yet we sill have a long way to go. We have accomplished our First Centenary Goal[4], and are now on a journey towards the Second Centenary Goal[5]. That is to build China into a modern socialist country in all respects. This goal, however, cannot be realized without modernizing agriculture and rural areas. We should pool our efforts to consolidate gains in poverty elimination with endeavors to revitalize[6] the countryside. In this way, we will help our rural people to live a modern life with a bright future.

The sole aims of the CPC in governance are to meet the needs of the people, and give its all in serving them and striving for their wellbeing. This has never changed throughout its hundred years of history. Numerous revolutionary martyrs[7] and forefathers sacrificed their lives for the cause or committed themselves to the reform and development of the country. We owe all our achievements to them.

We will stay true to the Party's original aspiration and founding mission and do solid work, generation after generation, so that by the centenary of the PRC in 2049, our nation will stand taller and stronger in the East and make a greater contribution to humanity.

Notes

1. This passage is an extract from *Xi Jinping: The Governance of China* Ⅳ, published by Foreign Languages Press in 2022.
2. terrain: a piece of ground having specific characteristics or military potential.
3. Loess Plateau refers to 黄土高原.
4. First Centenary Goal refers to "第一个百年奋斗目标".
5. Second Centenary Goal refers to "第二个百年奋斗目标".
6. revitalize: restore strength.
7. martyrs: one who suffers for the sake of principle.

Passage

Maintain World Peace and Stability[1]

Xi Jinping

"Stability brings a country prosperity while instability may well plunge it into poverty."[2] Security underpins development. Humanity is a community of indivisible security. A Cold War[3] mindset can only disrupt the global peace framework, hegemonism[4] and power politics can only endanger world peace, and confrontation between blocs can only exacerbate threats to security in the 21st century. All this has been proved time and again. To promote security for all the world, China proposes a Global Security Initiative[5]:

We should stay committed to the vision of common, comprehensive, cooperative and sustainable security, and work together to maintain world peace and security.

We should respect the sovereignty and territorial integrity of all countries, oppose interference[6] in internal affairs, and recognize the independent choice of development paths and social systems made by peoples of different countries.

We should abide by the purposes and principles of the UN Charter[7], reject the Cold War mentality, and oppose unilateralism[8], group politics and bloc rivalry.

We should address the legitimate security concerns of all countries, uphold the principle of indivisible security, build a balanced, effective and sustainable security architecture, and oppose any attempt by any country to ensure its own security at the expense of the security of others.

We should resolve differences and disputes between countries through dialogue, consultation and other peaceful means, support all efforts for peaceful settlement of crises, reject double standards, and oppose any abuse of unilateral sanctions[9] and long-arm jurisdiction[10].

We should maintain security in both traditional and non-traditional domains, and jointly resolve regional disputes and global issues such as terrorism, climate change, cybersecurity and biosecurity.

1. This passage is an extract from *Xi Jinping: The Governance of China* IV, published by Foreign Languages Press in 2022.

2. This is a quote from Guanzi, "治国常富,而乱国常贫。"

3. The Cold War was an ongoing political rivalry between the United States and the Soviet Union and their respective allies that developed after World War II.

4. hegemonism: control by the strongest and most powerful group, especially the strongest and most powerful country.

5. Global Security Initiative refers to 全球安全倡议.

6. interference: a policy of intervening in the affairs of other countries.

7. UN Charter: The Charter of the United Nations is the founding document of the United Nations. It was signed on 26 June 1945, in San Francisco, at the conclusion of the United Nations Conference on International Organization, and came into force on 24 October 1945.

8. unilateralism: the doctrine that nations should conduct their foreign affairs individualistically without the advice or involvement of other nations.

9. Unilateral sanction refers to the economic measures taken by one state to compel a change in the policy of another state.

10. Long-arm jurisdiction refers to the power of a court in one state to assert personal jurisdiction over a person in another state.

The Way Forward in the New Era[1]

Xi Jinping

As we look back on the journey the Party and the people have traveled since the 18th CPC National Congress[2] in 2012, we are all the more convinced of the following:

First, upholding overall Party leadership is the only way to advance socialism with Chinese characteristics[3]. As long as we uphold overall leadership by the Party and the authority of the Party Central Committee[4] and its centralized, unified leadership, we will be able to ensure stronger political cohesion and greater confidence in the Party and across the nation. We will be able to gather strength to keep to the correct political direction, work together to overcome difficulties, and remain the most reliable core of the nation when problems arise.

Second, socialism with Chinese characteristics is the only path to national rejuvenation[5]. As long as we remain committed to this path, we will be able to meet our people's aspirations for a better life and achieve common prosperity for all.

Third, solidarity is the only route for the Chinese people to achieve historic successes. We will surely overcome all challenges on our way forward and create new successes that will attract international acclaim[6], as long as we the Chinese people unite as one under the leadership of the Party, and have the courage and capacity to confront difficulties.

Fourth, implementing the new development philosophy[7] is the only way for China to grow stronger in the new era. As long as we fully, accurately and faithfully apply the new development philosophy, create a new development dynamic, promote high-quality development, and strengthen our self-reliance in science and technology, we will grow more competitive, achieve sustainable development, and keep hold of the initiative in an environment of fierce and increasing international competition.

Fifth, full and rigorous self-governance is the only way for the Party to maintain its vitality and realize the Second Centenary Goal. China's success hinges on our Party, so we must ensure that the Party practices strict self-governance in every respect. As long as we continue to carry forward the great founding spirit of the Party, have the courage to reform ourselves, remove all harmful elements that might damage the Party's progressive and wholesome nature, and treat all viruses that erode its health, we will be able to ensure that the Party does not change or betray its nature.

Notes

1. This passage is an extract from *Xi Jinping: The Governance of China* Ⅳ, published by Foreign Languages Press in 2022.
2. CPC National Congress refers to 中国共产党全国代表大会.
3. Socialism with Chinese characteristics refers to 中国特色社会主义.
4. Party Central Committee refers to 中国共产党中央委员会.
5. National rejuvenation refers to 民族复兴.
6. acclaim: enthusiastic approval.
7. The new development philosophy refers to 新发展理念.

Part Two
Vocabulary Building

Word List 1

	English	Chinese
1	head	在……的前头;掌管
2	code	密码;暗码
3	dial	拨号
4	loftily	高尚地;傲慢地
5	send for	召唤;派人去叫
6	tuck	把……塞入;把……夹入
7	barber	理发师
8	in accordance with	依照;与……一致
9	bemoan	惋惜;叹息
10	diary	日记

	English	Chinese
11	adjust	调整;调节
12	county	县
13	dispute	争论;辩论
14	mechanical	机械的;呆板的
15	slot	狭槽;投币口
16	light up	照亮
17	simplicity	简单;容易
18	indispensable	不可缺少的;绝对必要的
19	gets on my nerves	让我心烦;惹我厌烦
20	screen	屏幕
21	attic	阁楼;顶楼
22	crinkly	起皱的;卷曲的
23	fraction	分数;小部分
24	nonchalantly	冷淡地;漠不关心地
25	in no time	立刻;很快
26	sigh	叹了口气
27	speak for themselves	不言而喻;为自己辩护
28	infectious	传染的;有感染力的
29	pronounce	发音;正式宣布
30	proper	适当的;特有的
31	awfully	十分;非常
32	be supposed to	应该;被期望
33	insert	插入
34	punch	按键;拳头
35	superior	上级的;优秀的
36	neighbourhood	附近;街坊
37	at home in	熟悉;精通

	English	Chinese
38	laughter	笑;笑声
39	smart	聪明的
40	altogether	完全地;总共
41	calculate	计算;预测
42	plenty	很多
43	inspector	检查员;督察员
44	scornful	轻蔑的;鄙视的
45	regular	经常的;固定的
46	envy	羡慕;忌妒
47	harbor	海港;避难所
48	punch lines	(故事、戏剧、笑话等中的)妙语
49	disappointed	失望的;沮丧的
50	prepare	准备
51	run for	参选
52	champion	捍卫者
53	initiative	主动性;积极性
54	bring up	抚养
55	pantsuit	女式西装
56	signature	签名
57	combo	组合
58	extensive	广泛的
59	cross one's fingers	祈求成功
60	chill out	放松
61	beige	米黄色
62	single out	独立选择
63	adhere to	遵守
64	sartorial	服装的

	English	Chinese
65	distraction	分心
66	petty	琐碎的
67	aspirational	有抱负的
68	requisite	必需的
69	baggy	宽松的
70	show off	炫耀
71	disparity	差异
72	entirety	整体
73	lampoon	讽刺
74	bestow	授予
75	boo	嘘声
76	onslaught	猛攻
77	prejudice	偏见
78	ingrained	根深蒂固的
79	staple	主食
80	permeate	渗透
81	backlash	强烈反对
82	plunge	跳水
83	push the envelope	冒险尝试
84	rankle	激怒
85	clamp down	镇压
86	aftermath	后果
87	bubble	冒泡
88	mishmash	大杂烩
89	a host of	一大群
90	mishap	不幸
91	baffle	迷惑

	English	Chinese
92	leeway	余地
93	havoc	混乱
94	stifle	抑制
95	stodgy	乏味的
96	discriminate	歧视
97	religious	宗教的
98	dismiss	解雇
99	gussy up	打扮
100	ban	禁止

Word List 2

	English	Chinese
1	wave	挥手
2	terrific	极好的;了不起的
3	stylish	时髦的;流行的
4	spouse	配偶
5	routine	常规的;平常的
6	recipe	食谱
7	punctuality	准时性
8	priceless	无价的;极贵重的
9	panache	神气十足;派头
10	motorist	汽车驾驶员
11	aisle	走廊;过道
12	mood	心境;情绪
13	bar	条;棒

	English	Chinese
14	magic	魔法的;神奇的
15	barrel	快速移动
16	bellman	行李员
17	lipstick	口红;唇膏
18	irritation	恼怒;生气
19	bet	打赌;敢说
20	cherish	珍爱;抱有(希望)
21	do wonders for	创造奇迹
22	pull out	驶入主路;拔出
23	coworker	同事;合作者
24	compliment	赞美;恭维
25	insignificant	无关紧要的
26	image	形象;印象
27	melt away	消失;融掉
28	elevator	电梯
29	carry-on bag	手提行李;随身行李
30	take sb./sth. for granted	视为当然;认为某事当然
31	get away	离开;逃脱;出发
32	appreciate	欣赏;感激;领会
33	grateful	感谢的;感激的
34	put off	推迟;扔掉;阻止
35	infectious	传染性的;有感染力的
36	manner	态度;举止
37	manners	礼貌;礼仪
38	bother	打扰;烦扰
39	genuinely	真诚地;诚实地
40	apologize	谢罪;辩解

	English	Chinese
41	count	数数;重要;(被)正式接纳
42	value	评价;重视;估价
43	board	登上(火车、轮船或飞机)
44	generous	慷慨的;大量的
45	peer	同辈;同龄人
46	ethical	伦理的;道德的
47	innate	先天的;固有的
48	consciousness	清醒;观念
49	bystander	旁观者;局外人
50	push	推动;增加
51	bland	清淡的
52	edible	可食用的
53	in close proximity	靠近
54	ridicule	嘲笑
55	devour	狼吞虎咽
56	ritual	仪式
57	refer to	参考
58	distribution	分发
59	observe	观察
60	endow	赋予
61	presage	预示
62	elevate	提升
63	status	状态
64	secondary	次要的
65	substance	物质
66	peppery	辣的
67	butter up	奉承

	English	Chinese
68	trying	烦人的
69	range from...to...	范围从……到……
70	an excess of	过多的
71	trace back	追溯
72	complement	补充
73	masculine	男性的
74	spicy	辣的
75	deep-fry	油炸
76	metaphor	隐喻
77	assign	分配
78	fancy	喜欢
79	compose	组成
80	precede	领先
81	at the threshold of	在……的门槛上
82	intimacy	亲密
83	nuance	细微差别
84	pesticide	杀虫剂
85	to date	至今
86	conventional	传统的
87	organic	有机的
88	shell out	花钱
89	guideline	指南
90	compound	化合物
91	indestructible	难以破坏的
92	raillery	开玩笑
93	nutritional	营养的
94	shoddy	劣质的

	English	**Chinese**
95	delectable	美味的
96	seasoning	调味品
97	duality	二重性
98	rather	相当
99	connection	连接
100	leftover	剩余的

Word List 3

	English	**Chinese**
1	affect	使感染
2	bedridden	卧床不起的
3	carefree	无忧无虑的
4	emotion	感情
5	bond	关系
6	germ	细菌
7	bubble	气泡
8	invincible	不可战胜的
9	positive	积极的
10	lesion	损害
11	plague	瘟疫
12	outlook	见解；人生观
13	maintain	维持
14	mature	成熟的
15	mall	商场
16	break down	崩溃

	English	Chinese
17	strengthen	加强
18	unprotected	无防护的
19	stress	精神压力
20	react	回应
21	staff	全体职工
22	purple	紫色
23	blow off	(故意)失约；(故意)推脱
24	stuff	物品
25	for one's sake	为了某人
26	hang out	闲逛
27	hang up	挂断电话
28	hold in	克制
29	in a way	在某种程度上
30	keep in	控制感情
31	keep up	跟上
32	make sense	有意义
33	on one's own	独自地
34	rely on	依赖
35	stick it out	坚持到底
36	turn one's back on	背弃
37	exclusively	仅仅；排除其他地
38	high-profile	引人注目的
39	lethal	致命的
40	rash	皮疹
41	transfusion	输血
42	unsterilized	未经消毒的
43	immune	免疫

	English	Chinese
44	ward off	防止；避免
45	susceptible	易受影响的
46	pneumonia	肺炎
47	microorganism	微生物
48	intravenous	注入静脉的
49	impair	损害，削弱
50	fungal	真菌的
51	well-meaning	善意的
52	warn	警告
53	underground	地下的
54	notorious	臭名昭著的
55	resident	居民
56	City that Never Sleeps	不夜城
57	dilemma	困境
58	ambivalent	矛盾的
59	breakdown	崩溃
60	crumbling	破碎的
61	paralyze	使瘫痪
62	innocent	无辜的
63	randomly	随机地
64	hellish	地狱般的
65	indictment	控告
66	mixture	混合物
67	inefficient	低效的
68	sympathetic	同情的
69	swear by	以……名义发誓；对……发誓
70	small wonder	不足为奇

	English	Chinese
71	enduring	持久的
72	destination	目的地
73	try out	尝试
74	teeming	拥挤的
75	stratum	社会阶层
76	sport	(引人注目地)穿戴；炫耀
77	straphanger	(尤指拉住吊环)站立的乘客；公共交通乘客
78	deadlocked	梳着"骇人"长发绺的
79	disapprovingly	不赞同地
80	rub shoulders with	与(知名人士等)有交往；与……厮混在一起
81	epitomize	是……的典型
82	capture	捕捉
83	common	公共用地
84	dim	昏暗的
85	accomplice	共犯
86	bewildering	令人困惑的
87	glimpse	一瞥
88	essential	必要的
89	mobility	流动性
90	congestion	拥挤
91	antidote	解药
92	overshadow	使黯然失色
93	integral	不可或缺的
94	incorporate	合并
95	vertical	垂直的
96	versatility	多才多艺
97	escalate	升级

	English	Chinese
98	economical	经济的
99	permanent	永久的
100	fiscal	财政的

Word List 4

	English	Chinese
1	assortment	分类
2	elaborate	精心制作的
3	barely	仅仅
4	cute	精明的
5	atmosphere	气氛
6	chitchat	闲聊
7	birthstone	诞生石
8	bittersweet	苦中带甜的
9	fondly	天真地
10	recollection	记忆;回忆
11	generosity	慷慨大方
12	holly	冬青
13	relegate	使降级
14	gift-wrapped	包装精美的
15	hug	拥抱
16	perfunctory	敷衍的
17	popularity	流行
18	legible	清晰易读的
19	reminder	引起回忆的事物

	English	Chinese
20	surpass	超出;优于
21	rural	乡村的
22	signal	迹象;预示
23	shaped	具有某种形状的
24	ruby	红宝石
25	succession	一连串
26	represent	代表;象征
27	scrawl	马马虎虎地写
28	tease	取笑;戏弄
29	usher in	引进;开始
30	tulip	郁金香
31	put a lump in sb's throat	哽咽
32	valentine	情人卡;情人
33	bulletin board	布告板
34	postal service	邮政服务
35	give way to	被……代替
36	accomplish	完成
37	bolster	改善
38	commute	(乘公共汽车、火车、汽车等)上下班往返
39	detour	绕道
40	executive	有执行权的
41	grant	同意;批准
42	nail	钉牢;固定
43	thrifty	节约的
44	wobbly	摇摆的
45	unstinting	慷慨的
46	permanent	永久的

	English	Chinese
47	luxurious	奢侈的
48	heighten	加强
49	horizon	地平线
50	immigrate	（从外地）移居
51	patriarch	家长;族长
52	cradle	摇篮
53	crouch	蹲下
54	compensation	补偿
55	shade	阴影
56	weather-beaten	风吹雨打的
57	grazing	放牧
58	flock	群;群集
59	inhabit	居住于
60	splashing	溅水
61	charge	收费
62	milk	挤奶
63	stray into	迷路进入
64	abundance	丰富
65	contribute to	促成;有助于
66	environmental	环境的
67	controversial	有争议的
68	excavate	挖掘
69	giggle out	咯咯笑出声
70	die down	逐渐平息
71	encounter	遇到
72	hospitality	款待
73	shepherd	牧羊人

	English	Chinese
74	pile into	挤进
75	ramshackle	破旧的
76	partake in	参与
77	biodiversity	生物多样性
78	gesture	做手势
79	live off	靠……生活
80	in disbelief	不敢相信
81	mighty	强大的
82	bring about	导致
83	tend to	倾向于
84	survive	幸存
85	serve	服务
86	be bound to	必定
87	harness	利用
88	threshold	门槛
89	sustainability	可持续性
90	yawning	豁开的,裂开的
91	legacy	遗产;遗赠财物
92	die out	灭绝
93	boost	提升
94	status quo	现状
95	tourism	旅游业
96	virtuous	有道德的
97	grace	给……增色;莅临
98	erode	侵蚀
99	civilization	文明
100	company	陪伴

Word List 5

	English	Chinese
1	appeal	吸引力
2	corporation	公司
3	blond	金发女郎
4	contract	合同
5	colossal	巨大的
6	cease	停止
7	dumb	愚蠢的
8	furnishings	室内陈设
9	glamour	魅力
10	hit	很受欢迎的人或事物
11	ideal	理想的
12	hip	臀部
13	immortal	流芳百世的
14	entertainment	娱乐
15	intellectual	有才智的
16	peak	顶峰
17	magnet	有吸引力的
18	lease	租用
19	packed	拥挤的
20	palm-fringed	棕榈树环绕的
21	neighboring	邻近的
22	occasionally	偶尔
23	location	(电影的)外景拍摄地

	English	Chinese
24	script	电影剧本
25	tyrant	专横的人
26	toss	抛；掷
27	presidency	总统职位或任期
28	starlet	崭露头角的年轻演员
29	typecast	使（演员）一再扮演某类角色
30	site	地点
31	stunt	（尤指电影中的）特技表演
32	motion picture	电影
33	yacht	快艇
34	unscrupulous	无道德原则的
35	hold on a tight rein	牢牢控制
36	in vain	徒然
37	whatsoever	无论什么
38	interfere in	干涉
39	animated	栩栩如生的
40	celebrate	赞美；颂扬
41	creator	创造者
42	honor	给予表扬
43	profit	利润
44	ride	供乘骑的游乐设施
45	star	当主演
46	project	项目；方案
47	exploration	勘探
48	approve	批准
49	agricultural	农业的
50	anniversary	周年纪念日

	English	Chinese
51	hazardous	危险的
52	ATM（Automatic Teller Machine）	自动取款机
53	balance	余额
54	loan	贷款
55	debt	债务
56	figure out	弄清楚
57	hefty	庞大的
58	penalty	处罚
59	punitive	惩罚性的
60	wind up	结束
61	credit score	信用评分
62	far-reaching	影响深远的
63	sparkling	闪闪发光的
64	out of reach	无法达到
65	amass	积累
66	keep up with	跟上
67	ace	高手
68	in line with	符合
69	snag	障碍
70	land	着陆
71	saddle	负担
72	desperate	绝望的
73	go through	经历
74	defer	推迟
75	straighten out	理清,理顺
76	stun	震惊

	English	Chinese
77	cutoff	截止日期
78	slip	滑落
79	solicitation	教唆；引诱
80	account	账户
81	apply	申请
82	mask	掩盖
83	tout	兜售
84	bankruptcy	破产
85	back-and-forth	谈判
86	spiral	螺旋式上升
87	comprise	包含
88	probe	探究
89	boost	提升
90	dog	困扰
91	invisible	看不见的
92	lease	租赁
93	diligence	努力
94	pay off	偿清
95	cut back on	削减
96	inheritance	遗产
97	run up against	遭遇
98	elusive	难以捉摸的
99	frugality	节俭
100	brown-bagging	自带午餐

Word List 6

	English	Chinese
1	descend	下来；下降
2	alien	外国的
3	curl	卷发
4	agile	敏捷的
5	dazed	神志不清的
6	bungalow	平房
7	heritage	遗产
8	faded	褪色的
9	gruffness	冷淡
10	heed	留意
11	earthen	泥土做的
12	despise	鄙视
13	grub	翻找
14	desperate	极需要的；渴望的
15	household	一家人；家庭
16	immense	极大的
17	hypocrisy	伪善
18	indecision	优柔寡断
19	linger	流连；徘徊
20	martyr	烈士；殉道者
21	inestimable	难以估量的
22	mission	布道
23	pantry	食品储藏室
24	muddy	泥泞的

	English	Chinese
25	peril	严重危险
26	mouth	言不由衷地说
27	render	给予；提供
28	pious	道貌岸然的
29	obligation	义务；责任
30	peanut	花生
31	splash	泼溅着水行进；拍打着水游
32	rouse	唤醒
33	somber	昏暗的
34	sentimental	伤感的
35	thresh	使脱粒
36	treacherous	危险的
37	vendor	小贩
38	unctuous	谄媚的
39	voracious	（对信息、知识）渴求的
40	undiluted	纯洁的
41	wretched	不愉快的
42	zest	热情
43	make off	匆忙离开
44	on hand	在手边
45	stream	（光线）照射
46	solitary	孤单的
47	stool	凳子
48	sinister	险恶的；不祥的
49	indefatigable	不屈不挠的
50	binding	（书籍的）封皮
51	mobile	移动的

	English	Chinese
52	link	链接
53	mobility	流动性
54	figurative	比喻的
55	literal	字面的
56	strike	罢工
57	prospect	前景
58	reinvention	彻底改造
59	engineer	工程师
60	orientation	方向
61	confine	限制
62	fundamental	基本的
63	myriad	无数的
64	constant	不断的
65	built-in	内置的
66	transaction	交易
67	around the corner	即将来临
68	adept	熟练的
69	transmit	传输
70	staggering	令人震惊的
71	inextricably	不可分割地
72	immerse	沉浸
73	homogenization	同质化
74	tap	轻拍
75	access	接入
76	exotic	异国的
77	erode	侵蚀
78	celebrity	名人

Part Two Vocabulary Building

	English	Chinese
79	break out of	逃脱……
80	advent	出现
81	navigate	导航
82	grapple with	努力克服（或解决、完成、对付）……
83	contra	反对
84	website	网站
85	vast	广阔的
86	cutting-edge	尖端的
87	targeted	有针对性的
88	lose sight of	忽视……
89	avatar	（尤指电脑游戏或社交媒体中的）用户头像
90	tangible	有形的
91	fuel	燃料
92	foresee	预见
93	pursue	追求
94	prohibit	禁止
95	yield	产生
96	virtual	虚拟的
97	plight	困境
98	compelling	令人信服的
99	immigrate	移民
100	global positioning system	全球定位系统

Word List

	English	Chinese
1	cling	抓紧

71

	English	Chinese
2	blessed	有福的
3	alternative	可供替代的
4	bee	(为进行社区工作、竞赛等举行的)聚会
5	bow	蝴蝶结
6	clutch	紧握
7	anticipate	期盼
8	glinting	闪闪发光的
9	drawl	(拉长调子)慢吞吞地说
10	complain	抱怨
11	confide	(向某人)吐露隐私
12	fateful	命中注定的
13	glamorous	特别有魅力的
14	crash	撞车;碰撞
15	indiscriminate	随意的
16	indebted	感激的
17	intensely	极其
18	pocket	(与周围不同的)小组织,小区域
19	lunge	猛冲
20	jolt	颠簸
21	lament	对……感到悲痛
22	procedure	程序
23	reassure	使……安心
24	slam	砰地关上
25	rocky	问题成堆的;困难重重的
26	screech	发出刺耳声
27	soothing	慰藉的
28	soulful	深情的

	English	Chinese
29	roller coaster	过山车
30	squeeze	挤压;捏
31	swerve	突然转向;急转弯
32	thundercloud	雷雨云
33	unbolt	拔掉门闩;打开
34	transfer	转乘
35	witness	目睹（某事发生）
36	get in	到达
37	pull oneself together	镇定下来
38	strap in	使系好安全带
39	ascertain	查明;弄清
40	bow	船头
41	disengage	脱离;解脱
42	lateral	侧面的;横向的
43	overhang	悬垂
44	rig	(给船只)装配帆及索具等
45	oar	船桨
46	strap	用带子系
47	zenith	天顶
48	life preserver	救生用具
49	steward	乘务员
50	stateroom	特等客舱
51	stunt	噱头;作秀
52	box office	票房
53	genre	类型
54	director	导演
55	Hollywood	好莱坞

	English	Chinese
56	buddy-cop film	警匪片
57	soft power	软实力
58	poach	挖（其他公司雇员等）
59	transformation	转变
60	indicate	表明
61	tie	结合
62	exclusive	独家的
63	liberalization	自由化
64	mandatory	强制性的
65	multiplex	多厅影院
66	dramatically	戏剧性地
67	shoot	拍摄
68	privatization	私有化
69	distribution	分配
70	match	匹配
71	integrate	整合
72	studio	影片制片厂
73	export	出口
74	globalization	全球化
75	in turn	反过来
76	imperialism	帝国主义
77	anchor	主持人
78	top	顶级的
79	martial art	武术
80	defy	违抗
81	release	发行
82	high-end	高端的

Part Two Vocabulary Building

	English	Chinese
83	differ from	与……不同
84	glamour	魅力
85	contribute to	有助于
86	transnational	跨国的
87	blockbuster	轰动一时的大片
88	balloon	膨胀
89	venue	场所
90	audience	观众
91	aim	目标
92	disavow	否认
93	distinct	明显的
94	break down	分解
95	claim	声称
96	surge	激增
97	entice	引诱
98	mean	意味着
99	spur	刺激
100	mitigation	缓解

Word List

	English	Chinese
1	bias	偏见；偏向
2	ceremony	仪式；典礼
3	commonplace	平凡的
4	connotation	内涵意义

	English	Chinese
5	denote	标志;预示
6	dominate	支配;统治
7	encode	为……编码
8	destruction	摧毁
9	endow	赋予
10	disparity	差异;悬殊
11	enforce	强迫;迫使
12	discerning	有识别力的
13	exalted	地位高的
14	harbor	怀有
15	ill-tempered	脾气暴躁的
16	feminine	阴性的
17	genetics	遗传学
18	grace	恩宠
19	implement	使生效
20	oriented	以……为方向的
21	nuance	细微差别
22	inherently	本质上
23	masculine	阳性的
24	linguistic	语言的
25	internally	在内部
26	mechanism	机制;方法
27	perpetuate	使永久或持续
28	scoff	嘲笑;讥讽
29	qualify	修饰;限定
30	prejudice	使怀有（或产生）偏见
31	shrew	悍妇

	English	Chinese
32	shrewd	精明的
33	unmerited	不配得的
34	scolding	斥责;训斥
35	subservience	从属;屈从
36	supremacy	至高无上
37	vicious	凶猛危险的
38	yield	提供;产生
39	identify sb. With sth.	认为某人与……相关
40	wed	结婚;娶;嫁
41	bare	使露出
42	beckon	招手示意
43	diversity	多样性
44	bargain	讨价还价
45	elusive	难以发现的
46	execute	执行;实施
47	hail	跟……打招呼
48	hook	钩住
49	nonverbal	非言语的
50	oriental	东方人的
51	urbanization	城市化
52	suburb	郊区
53	lampoon	讽刺
54	haunt	困扰
55	torch	火把
56	resident	居民
57	epitomize	成为……的典范(或典型)
58	boast	自夸

	English	Chinese
59	downtown	市中心
60	emerging	新兴的
61	sprawl	蔓延
62	car-oriented	以汽车为导向的
63	empty	空的
64	edge	边缘
65	metropolis	大都市
66	speed up	加速
67	flee	逃离
68	zone	区域
69	mass affluence	大规模富裕
70	density	密度
71	hectare	公顷
72	collapse	崩溃
73	sociable	社交的
74	squalor	肮脏
75	privacy	隐私
76	dignified	庄重的
77	aspire	渴望
78	detractor	（恶意）批评者
79	progress	进步
80	Hispanic	西班牙（人）的
81	blend	混合
82	decay	衰败
83	overlook	忽视
84	revive	复兴
85	impose	强加

	English	Chinese
86	urbanite	城市居民
87	suburbanite	郊区居民
88	alleviate	缓解
89	barmy	傻乎乎的;疯疯癫癫的
90	astronomical	天文数字的
91	insistence	坚持
92	strip	剥夺
93	chunk	大块
94	appalling	令人震惊的
95	rampant	猖獗的
96	constrain	限制
97	tot	总计
98	criss-cross	纵横交错
99	offset	抵消
100	hurdle	障碍

Word List

	English	Chinese
1	access	通道;通路
2	boundary	边界;界限;分界线
3	ego	自我价值感;自尊心
4	fascism	法西斯主义
5	instantly	立即;马上
6	manicurist	指甲美容师;护手师
7	rear	后部

	English	Chinese
8	stroke	中风
9	threaten	预示凶兆;有……危险
10	keep apart	(使)分开
11	assure	断言;使确信;向……保证
12	consequence	结果;后果
13	endure	忍耐;忍受
14	fatal	致命的
15	intuition	直觉
16	miff	使恼怒
17	rescuer	救援者;营救者
18	subtitle	(电影或电视上的)字幕
19	tumor	肿瘤
20	move on	开始做(别的事);换话题
21	authorize	批准;授权
22	console	安慰;抚慰;慰藉
23	epiphany	顿悟
24	flee	迅速离开;逃避,逃跑
25	lump	肿块;隆起
26	occupation	侵占;占领期
27	slur	含混不清地说话
28	suicidal	有自杀倾向的
29	undergo	经历;经受
30	set apart	留出;拨出(专用)
31	beneficiary	受益者;受惠人
32	deplorable	糟透的;令人震惊的;令人愤慨的
33	establish	建立;创立;设立
34	gurney	(医院中推送病人用的)轮床

	English	Chinese
35	malignant	恶性的
36	poignant	令人沉痛的;悲惨的
37	spinal	脊柱的;脊髓的
38	surgery	外科手术;外科学
39	wreckage	残骸
40	stretch out	伸展
41	breast	(女子的)乳房
42	diagnostic	诊断的;判断的
43	eventually	最后;终于
44	helicopter	直升机
45	manicure	修剪指甲;指甲护理
46	psychiatrist	精神病学家;精神科医生
47	striking	引人注目的;异乎寻常的
48	therapist	(某治疗法的)治疗专家
49	wrist	手腕;腕关节
50	be wrapped up in	专心致志于;完全沉浸于
51	exposed	暴露的
52	proficient	熟练的
53	medium	媒介;中等
54	bizarre	奇异的
55	umpteen	大量的
56	elasticity	弹性
57	messy	凌乱的
58	barriers to entry	进入(市场)壁垒
59	galore	大量的
60	a host of	许多;一大群
61	Internettery	互联网术语

	English	Chinese
62	computerese	计算机术语
63	phonebabble	手机术语
64	fogy	老顽固;守旧落伍的人
65	neologism	新词;新义
66	angst	焦虑;忧虑
67	laisser-faire	放任政策的;不干涉主义的
68	triumph	胜利;成功
69	have little to do with	与……关系不大
70	colony	殖民地
71	farther afield	去远处;在远方
72	alliance	联盟;同盟
73	accommodating	乐于助人的
74	friction	摩擦;冲突
75	merit	优点;价值
76	converse	相反;对话
77	repository	存储库;仓库
78	engulf	吞没;包围
79	lament	悲叹;哀悼
80	mutation	变异;突变
81	aspire	渴望;立志
82	lingua franca	通用语;交际语
83	encroach	侵占;侵犯
84	far from alone	绝非孤例;并非孤独
85	go into effect	生效
86	oblige	强迫;迫使
87	oppressive	压迫的;沉重的
88	legacy	遗留问题;后遗症

	English	Chinese
89	exterminate	消灭;根除
90	go out of business	倒闭;停业
91	outright	彻底的;明确的
92	extinction	灭绝;消亡
93	paradoxically	自相矛盾
94	multilingualism	多语言能力
95	monoglot	单一语言使用者
96	Esperanto	世界语
97	dubious	可疑的
98	commonplace	老生常谈
99	brush up	温习;复习
100	alloy	合金

Word List

	English	Chinese
1	admonition	警告;告诫
2	afflict	折磨;使痛苦
3	bang	突然的巨响
4	bundle up	使穿暖和
5	cripple	跛子;瘸子
6	dismiss	去除;消除;摒除
7	enormity	巨大;深远影响;严重性
8	frustrated	懊丧的;懊恼的;沮丧的
9	gauge	依据;尺度;标准
10	hobble	蹒跚;跛行

	English	Chinese
11	affair	不寻常之物;难描述的东西
12	aid	帮助;助手;辅助物
13	blowout	爆胎
14	clank	铿铿声;当当声
15	crutch	腋杖
16	driveway	私人车道
17	frail	瘦弱的
18	fumble	笨手笨脚地做
19	gusty	阵阵劲吹的;刮风的
20	honk	鸣喇叭
21	horn	喇叭
22	install	安装;设置
23	jack	千斤顶;起重器
24	overflow	漫出;溢出
25	penetrate	穿过;进入
26	prophet	先知;预言家
27	shoulder	路肩;紧急停车道
28	slash	(用利器)砍;劈;割
29	spent	筋疲力尽的
30	sweep	(感受或情感)突然袭来
31	indifference	漠不关心
32	interval	间隔;间隙
33	jerk	急拉;猛推;猝然一动
34	paralyze	使瘫痪;使麻痹
35	peninsula	半岛
36	scriptural	《圣经》的;依据《圣经》的
37	slacken	放慢;变萧条

	English	Chinese
38	slick	滑溜溜的
39	split-level	错层式的
40	thump	步履沉重地走
41	tilt	(使)倾斜；倾侧
42	utterly	全然；彻底地
43	whatsoever	任何；无论什么
44	yardstick	衡量标准；准绳
45	be all set	准备就绪
46	be inclined to	倾向于；很可能
47	dirt road	土路
48	flat tire	漏了气的车胎
49	hold on to	抓紧；不放开
50	peer at	仔细看；凝视
51	subsidiary	子公司
52	esteemed	受人尊敬的
53	supply	供应；提供
54	recommend	推荐；建议
55	be wary about	对……谨慎
56	awkward	尴尬的；笨拙的
57	lay sb. open to	使某人遭受批评；置某人于尴尬处境
58	accusation	指控；控告
59	favoritism	偏袒；偏爱
60	corruption	腐败；贪污
61	put out	生产；制造
62	bid	出价；投标
63	quack	庸医；骗子
64	ditch	抛弃；丢弃

	English	Chinese
65	abrasive	粗糙的;粗鲁的
66	portray	描绘;表现
67	soothing	安抚的;舒缓的
68	yell at	对……大吼大叫
69	over the top	过火的;夸张的
70	subordinate	下属;部下
71	counterpart	对应的人;相对应的物
72	prematurely	过早地;提前
73	underlying	潜在的;基础的
74	ethnocentricity	民族中心主义
75	display	展示;显示
76	appraisal	评估;鉴定
77	gamut	整个范围;音阶
78	confront	面对;对抗
79	initial	最初的;开始的
80	lay out	摆放;布置
81	characterize	描述;刻画
82	arise from	由……引起
83	preliminary	初步的;准备阶段的
84	priority	优先权;重点
85	confrontational	对抗的
86	nurturance	培育;养育
87	conciliatory	安抚的;抚慰的
88	intermediary	中介;调解人
89	circumvent	规避
90	delegate	代表
91	bureaucratic	官僚的;官僚主义的

	English	Chinese
92	autonomy	自治;自治权
93	constitute	构成;组成
94	tactfulness	圆通;老练
95	practitioner	(尤指医学或法律界的)从业者
96	heterogeneity	多样性;异质性
97	recognize	认可;承认
98	multicultural	多元文化的
99	bottle up	抑制(感受或情感)
100	provoke	激怒;引发

Word List 11

	English	Chinese
1	virtue	优点,长处;美德
2	worship	热爱;爱慕;崇拜
3	convince	说服;劝服
4	work out	锻炼身体;做运动
5	jog	慢步长跑(尤指锻炼)
6	delay	推迟;(故意)拖延
7	aging	变老;老化
8	devil	魔鬼;魔王
9	dread	畏惧;担心
10	distinct	明显的;确切的
11	ambiguous	模棱两可的;有歧义的
12	be apt to	倾向于
13	be obsessed with	痴迷于;心神不宁

	English	Chinese
14	feverishly	兴奋地;狂热地
15	megadose	大剂量(药品、维生素等)
16	wiry	(人)瘦而结实的
17	muscular	肌肉发达的
18	diet	节食
19	constantly	总是;经常地
20	waist	腰;腰部
21	plead	恳求;乞求
22	fall apart	崩溃;瓦解;破碎
23	loose-fitting	(衣服)宽松的,肥大的
24	blazer	(常带俱乐部、学校、运动队等的颜色或徽章的)运动夹克
25	tailor	定做(衣服);迎合,使适应
26	adolescent	青少年
27	freak	(行为、外表、想法)怪异的人
28	in general	通常;一般而言
29	agony	(精神/身体)极大痛苦
30	slice	(切下的食物)薄片
31	in the mood	心情好;兴致勃勃
32	at the mercy of	支配
33	embarrass	窘迫;使难堪
34	await	将发生在(某人身上)
35	pursue	继续探讨(或追究、从事)
36	carefree	无忧无虑的;无牵挂的
37	unsettling	令人不安(或紧张、担忧)的
38	take up with	开始结交(尤指名声不好的人)
39	resent	怨恨;憎恶

	English	Chinese
40	critical	极其重要的;关键的
41	accomplished	熟练的;非常优秀的
42	contrast	差异;对比
43	sanity	精神正常;明智
44	self-identity	自我认同
45	quirk	怪癖;怪异的性格（或行为）
46	keep score	在比赛中记分;做记录
47	saint	圣人般的人（指特别善良、仁爱或有耐性的人）
48	contradict	相矛盾;反驳
49	premise	前提;假设
50	contentment	满足;满意
51	convey	传达;表达
52	faculty	能力;才能
53	justification	理由;辩解
54	preserve	保护;保存
55	zest	热情;兴致
56	impart	传授;给予
57	arise from	起立;起床
58	be invested with	被赋予;具备
59	be divorced from	与……脱离关系
60	illuminate	阐明;启示
61	elicit	引出;引起
62	apply to	适用于;应用到
63	be consistent with	与……一致
64	in great measure	在很大程度上
65	feeble	虚弱的;无力的
66	act on	对……起作用

	English	Chinese
67	pedant	书呆子;卖弄学问者
68	weld	焊接;结合
69	flinch	畏缩;退缩
70	assertion	主张;断言
71	confrontation	对抗;冲突
72	scatter	分散;散布
73	temperate	温和的;适度的
74	interlocking	相互交织的;相互连接的
75	complex	复杂的
76	construe	解释;理解
77	binding force	维系力;束缚力
78	evoke	唤起;引发
79	discipline	纪律;学科
80	by reason of	由于;因为
81	obstinacy	顽固;固执
82	derive from	源自;来自
83	evaluation	评估;评价
84	pass into	进入;转变为
85	hamper	阻碍;妨碍
86	endeavor	努力;尽力
87	novice	新手;初学者
88	carry out	执行;实施
89	obedience	服从;顺从
90	prolonged	长时间的;持久的
91	dull	枯燥的;乏味的
92	underlie	构成……的基础
93	apprenticeship	学徒工作;学徒期

	English	Chinese
94	drudgery	苦工;苦差事
95	issue in	导致;引起
96	blind rule of thumb	盲目的经验法则
97	acquisition	获得;得到
98	grapple with	努力理解;尽力解决
99	ambiguous	模棱两可的;含糊不清的
100	pore over	钻研;仔细阅读

Word List

	English	Chinese
1	norm	标准
2	shift	(情况、意见、政策等)变换
3	eligibility	资格;合格
4	inadequacy	不胜任;缺乏信心
5	repute	名誉;名声
6	essence	本质;实质;精髓
7	offset	抵消,弥补,补偿
8	go under	破产
9	go broke	破产
10	shrug away	摆脱;不理会
11	perspective	态度;观点
12	put sth. in perspective	正确判断
13	take sth. at face value	相信表面
14	be apt to	倾向于……
15	misleading	误导的;引入歧途的

	English	Chinese
16	transcript	学生成绩报告单
17	proficiency	熟练;精通;娴熟
18	conventional	传统的;习惯的
19	correspond to	相一致;符合
20	retain	保持;持有;保留
21	assumption	假定;假设
22	indicate	标明;显示
23	fuzzy	混乱的;含糊不清的
24	character	品质;性格;(地方的)特点
25	humor	性情;气质;幽默
26	characteristic	特征;特点;品质
27	species	种;物种
28	curriculum	(学校等的)全部课程
29	garment	(一件)衣服
30	underneath	在……底下;隐藏(掩盖)在下面
31	ritual	程序;礼节;宗教仪式
32	academic	教学的;学业的
33	make a point of	重视;特别注意
34	frequent	常去,常到(某处)
35	swap	交换(东西)
36	flunk	给(某人)不及格
37	oddly	古怪地;怪异地
38	resent	愤恨;感到气愤
39	gear	齿轮;传动装置
40	coercive	强制的;胁迫的
41	semester	学期
42	hew	砍;劈

	English	Chinese
43	knit	紧密结合；紧凑
44	coordinate	坐标
45	irrelevant	无关紧要的；不相关的
46	complex	难懂的；费解的
47	rank	（尤指较高的）地位，级别
48	permanently	永久地；长期不变地
49	define	下定义
50	hamper	妨碍；阻碍
51	whisk	搅拌；迅速移动
52	scoot	快速移动；溜走
53	peel off	剥离；脱下
54	drape	悬挂；覆盖
55	swivel seat	转椅；旋转座椅
56	celebrated	著名的；知名的
57	legendary	传奇的；传说的
58	take-no-prisoners	无情的；残酷的
59	at any cost	不惜一切代价；无论如何
60	bedevil	困扰；折磨
61	stutter	结巴；口吃
62	vulnerable	脆弱的；易受伤的
63	untouched	未触动的；未受影响的
64	personify	使具体化；使人格化
65	deliver	交付；送达
66	chieftain	酋长；首领
67	tumble	摔倒；滚动
68	unforgiving	无情的；严酷的
69	domino	多米诺骨牌；连锁反应

	English	Chinese
70	keenly	敏锐地;热切地
71	old-line	传统的;老牌的
72	astutely	精明地;机敏地
73	acquisition	收购
74	emerging	新兴的;崛起的
75	wield	行使;运用
76	subsidiary	辅助的
77	appraisal	评估;鉴定
78	gamut	全部范围;音域
79	confront	质疑,质问(某人的行为或权威)
80	initial	(名字的)首字母
81	lay out	布置;安排
82	characterize	描述;刻画
83	arise from	上升;升起
84	preliminary	初步的;预备的
85	priority	优先权;重点
86	confrontational	想吵架(或打架)的
87	nurturance	培养;养育
88	conciliatory	调和的;调解的
89	intermediary	中间人;调解人
90	circumvent	绕行
91	delegate	参会人员
92	bureaucratic	专横的;武断的
93	autonomy	自主;自主权
94	constitute	构成;组成
95	tactfulness	策略;手段
96	practitioner	从事者;实践者

	English	Chinese
97	heterogeneity	多种多样;各种各样
98	recognize	认识;认出
99	multicultural	多种族文化的
100	bottle up	封锁（敌人等）

Word List

	English	Chinese
1	abstract	摘要;概要
2	abundant	大量的;丰盛的;充裕的
3	attest	证实;是……的证据
4	breed	饲养;培育（动植物）
5	coastline	海岸线;沿海地带
6	combat	防止;减轻
7	consciousness	觉察;感觉;意识
8	consumption	消耗;消耗量
9	curb	控制;抑制
10	decade	十年
11	deforestation	毁林;滥伐森林
12	drought	久旱;旱灾
13	excess	附加的;过度的
14	fend	抵挡;挡开;避开
15	fertilizer	肥料
16	fossil	化石
17	gasoline	汽油
18	greenhouse	温室,暖房

	English	Chinese
19	hemisphere	（地球的）半球
20	hurricane	飓风
21	impact	巨大影响；强大作用
22	journal	报纸；刊物；杂志
23	latitude	纬度
24	microwave	微波炉
25	mitigate	减轻；缓和
26	moderate	适度的；中等的
27	particle	颗粒
28	periodical	（学术）期刊
29	peruse	细读；研读
30	primarily	主要地；跟本地
31	radiation	辐射的热（或能量等）
32	recession	退后；撤回
33	region	地区；区域；地方
34	section	节；段；部分
35	spark	引发；触发
36	speculate	推测；猜测；推断
37	thermal	热的；热量的
38	windshield	挡风玻璃
39	carbon dioxide	二氧化碳
40	illusion	错觉；幻觉
41	energetic	精力充沛的；充满活力的
42	worship	热爱；爱慕；崇拜
43	critical	极其重要的；关键的
44	stroke	中风
45	ego	自我价值感；自尊心

	English	Chinese
46	compromise	妥协（或折中）方案
47	profound	深切的;深远的
48	frustrated	懊丧的;懊恼的;沮丧的
49	enrage	激怒;使暴怒
50	with an air of	带着……的样子
51	sprout	发芽;萌芽
52	league table	积分榜;排行榜
53	wealthscape	财富格局
54	decree	法令;判决
55	baron	男爵;巨头
56	spectator	观众;旁观者
57	competitive	竞争的;有竞争力的
58	fall off	下降;减少
59	shoot up	迅速上升;飙升
60	seesaw	跷跷板;摇摆不定
61	yacht	游艇;帆船
62	silver-tongued	口若悬河的;能言善辩的
63	source	来源;起源
64	threshold	门槛;阈值
65	plutocrat	富豪;财阀
66	bank balance	银行余额
67	obsess	迷恋;困扰
68	cruise	巡航;航行
69	dazzle	使惊叹;使目眩
70	commission	委托;佣金
71	luxury	奢侈品;豪华
72	scorecard	记分卡

	English	Chinese
73	signifier	符号;标记
74	make for	有助于;导致
75	rally	集会;团结
76	adversarial	对抗的;敌对的
77	overestimate	高估
78	antique	古董
79	bid	努力争取;企图获得
80	trace back to	追溯到
81	invoke	引用;援引
82	tame	驯服的;温顺的
83	excess	过量;过度
84	rein in	控制;约束
85	elite	精英;掌权人物
86	bunch	一束;一群
87	one-upmanship	胜人一筹的伎俩
88	magnate	大亨;巨头
89	demolish	拆除;毁坏
90	barbaric	野蛮的;残忍的
91	predecessor	前任;前辈
92	frenzy	狂热;狂怒
93	cram	填鸭式教育;填塞
94	diverse	多样的;不同的
95	inordinately	过度地;异常地
96	foible	弱点;小缺点
97	eclipse	日食;月食
98	amass	积累;聚集
99	scale up	增大,扩大(规模或数量)
100	in return for	作为回报;作为交换

Word List

	English	Chinese
1	mobile	可移动的
2	banner	横幅
3	budget	预算
4	cardinal	最重要的
5	catatonic	紧张型精神分裂症的
6	certificate	证明
7	chin	下巴
8	dedicate	把……奉献给
9	deliberately	故意
10	disapprove	不赞成
11	exhale	呼出
12	inhale	吸入
13	feature	特写,专题节目
14	felicity	幸福
15	fiction	小说
16	flawless	完美的
17	force	力量大的人或事
18	heighten	(使)加强,提高
19	inherent	固有的;内在的
20	insatiability	不知足
21	issue	发给;供给
22	knave	无赖
23	laxative	泻药
24	patriotism	爱国主义

	English	Chinese
25	patriotic	爱国的
26	perception	感知
27	perpetual	不间断的
28	pursue	追求
29	pursuit	追求
30	release	公开;发布
31	sake	由于;为了
32	tablet	药片
33	therapy	治疗
34	torture	(精神上或肉体上的)折磨
35	torment	(尤指精神上的)折磨
36	underline	强调
37	highlight	强调
38	uplifting	令人振奋的
39	discipline	纪律;自制力
40	possession	拥有
41	vague	模糊的
42	approach	接近
43	strap	捆绑
44	melt	熔化;融化
45	extreme	极大的;极度的
46	ideal	理想的;最佳的
47	spiritual	精神的;心灵的
48	rapt	全神贯注的;入迷的
49	contemplation	沉思;冥想
50	devout	虔诚的;衷心的
51	challenge	挑战

Part Two Vocabulary Building

	English	Chinese
52	tidal wave	海啸;潮汐
53	creep	蔓延;爬行
54	ooze	渗出;渗漏
55	manifestly	明显地;明白地
56	homogenous	同质的;同构的
57	sickly	病态的;不健康的
58	imbibe	喝,饮(酒等)
59	abrupt	突然的;意外的
60	dump	倾倒;抛弃
61	seductive	诱人的;迷人的
62	blatantly	明目张胆地;公然地
63	superficial	肤浅的;表面的
64	exhilarating	令人兴奋的;使人振奋的
65	oppressive	压迫的;沉重的
66	mingle	混合;交融
67	excessive	过度的;过量的
68	undermine	逐渐削弱(信心、权威等)
69	ever-stronger	日益强大的;越来越强的
70	conscious	有意识的;自觉的
71	justify	证明……正当
72	dub	配音;称呼
73	pervasive	普遍的;弥漫的
74	middle ground	中庸之道;折中方案
75	overwhelming	压倒性的
76	psyche	心理;灵魂
77	disorientation	迷失方向;迷惑
78	invasion	入侵;侵略

	English	Chinese
79	domineering	盛气凌人的;专横的
80	hegemony	霸权;霸权国
81	veritable	真正的;确实的
82	propagate	繁殖;传播
83	far-reaching	广泛的
84	commodity	商品;物品
85	crucible	坩埚;严峻考验
86	bombard	轰炸;连续攻击
87	discard	丢弃;抛弃
88	cohesion	凝聚力;团结
89	cost-effective	性价比高的;划算的
90	resemble	类似
91	integration	整合;融合
92	corrosive	腐蚀性的;侵蚀性的
93	solidarity	团结
94	displace	取代;替换
95	assortment	各种各样;品种繁多
96	archetype	原型;典型
97	automate	自动化;使自动化
98	veer	改变方向
99	go public	上市;公开
100	parachute	降落伞

Word List 15

	English	Chinese
1	abound	大量存在

	English	**Chinese**
2	appropriate	盗用；挪用
3	authorities	当局；当权者
4	beckon	吸引
5	boost	增长
6	canvas	帆布
7	commodity	商品
8	confine	限制
9	craze	狂热
10	dangle	悬垂
11	decoration	装饰品
12	demonstrable	明显的
13	ditch	沟
14	dye	给……染色
15	emigrate	移居国外
16	ensuing	接着发生的
17	equality	平等
18	exaggerate	夸张
19	faulty	不完美的
20	gang	一帮
21	gimmick	花招
22	girth	腰围
23	haul	拖；拉；拽
24	hook	钩住
25	idiosyncratic	怪异的
26	indigo	靛青
27	legitimate	正当合理的
28	loop	环形

	English	Chinese
29	marginal	小的
30	mean-tempered	易怒的
31	outlive	比……持久
32	pacify	使平静
33	patent	获得专利权
34	profitable	有利润的
35	proletarian	无产者的
36	prosper	繁荣
37	rigor	严格
38	rivet	铆钉
39	rugged	结实的
40	slit	切开
41	sole	唯一的
42	stuff	填满
43	sturdy	结实的
44	sundries	杂物
45	surf	激浪；拍岸浪花
46	symbol	象征
47	thereafter	之后
48	tribute	体现
49	ubiquitous	无所不在的
50	convert	转换
51	golden rule	黄金法则
52	set foot on	踏上
53	be inundated with	被淹没；充斥着
54	preamble	序言
55	allegedly	据称；据说

	English	Chinese
56	violation	违反;侵犯
57	stun	使震惊;使目瞪口呆
58	make a comeback	复出;东山再起
59	scandal	丑闻;丑行
60	implement	实施;执行
61	implicate	牵涉
62	revoke	废除
63	hack	非法侵入(他人的计算机系统)
64	consistency	一致性;连贯性
65	expulsion	开除;驱逐
66	expel	开除;驱逐
67	appeal	上诉;呼吁
68	deliberate	故意的;慎重的
69	integrity	正直;诚信
70	hectic	忙碌的;繁忙的
71	embezzle	盗用;侵占
72	come to light	曝光;被发现
73	be made up of	由……组成
74	tie	领带;关系
75	be guilty of	犯有……罪
76	honor code	荣誉准则
77	at length	详尽地;长时间地
78	foolproof	不会出毛病的;万无一失的
79	cheat	作弊;欺骗
80	cornerstone	基石;基础
81	affirm	肯定;断言
82	discourage	阻止;使沮丧

	English	Chinese
83	average	平均的;一般的
84	dismiss	解雇;驳回
85	be accused of	被指控;被指责
86	initially	最初;起初
87	penalty	处罚;刑罚
88	faculty	全体教师
89	be informed of	被告知
90	be confined to	局限于
91	uphold	维护;支持
92	get ahead	领先;胜过
93	inexplicable	费解的;无法解释的
94	commitment	承诺;委托
95	underestimate	低估;看轻
96	take advantage of	利用;占便宜
97	diagnose	诊断;判断
98	self-confidence	自信;自信心
99	commission	委员会
100	determination	决心;决定

Word List 16

	English	Chinese
1	access	通道
2	adjustment	调整
3	afford	买得起
4	approximate	接近

	English	Chinese
5	click	使发出咔嗒声
6	complacent	自满的
7	compromise	妥协方案
8	conference	会议
9	despair	绝望
10	enable	使能够
11	essential	完全必要的
12	facilitate	促进
13	head-on	正面的
14	hence	因此
15	hover	靠近
16	hybrid	混合的
17	intercultural	不同文化间的
18	involve	包含
19	label	贴标签
20	long	渴望
21	mentality	心态
22	messaging	消息传递
23	misgiving	疑虑;顾虑
24	mock	嘲弄
25	monolingual	单语的
26	oasis	绿洲
27	overlook	忽略
28	profound	巨大的
29	provided	如果
30	regarding	关于
31	remote	偏远的

	English	Chinese
32	reveal	显出
33	significant	有意义的
34	spectrum	光谱
35	staple	主要的
36	swallow	吞下
37	unsurmountable	无法克服的
38	wonder	想知道
39	peril	危险
40	uneasiness	不安
41	image	形象
42	boundary	边界
43	democracy	民主
44	inevitable	不可避免的
45	negotiate	协商
46	accordingly	相应地
47	familiar	熟悉的
48	desert	沙漠
49	homesick	想家的
50	untranslatability	不可译性
51	ignore	忽视
52	fundamental	根本的
53	far-flung	遥远的;广泛分布的
54	seismic	地震的;重大的
55	take place	发生;举行
56	discovery	发现;探索
57	rationalism	理性主义;唯理主义
58	nurture	培养;抚育

	English	Chinese
59	aesthetic	审美的；美学的
60	secular	世俗的；非宗教的
61	fragmented	碎片化的；分散的
62	decisive	决定性的；果断的
63	religious	宗教的；虔诚的
64	anticipate	预期；预料
65	flourish	繁荣；兴盛
66	ultimately	最终；最后
67	give birth to	产生；引起
68	reflect	反映；体现
69	flowering	开花时节；鼎盛时期
70	interdependent	相互依存的；相互关联的
71	ceramics	制陶艺术
72	intricate	复杂的；错综复杂的
73	stipulate	规定；明确要求
74	opulence	富饶；富裕
75	lavish	奢华的；慷慨的
76	pre-eminence	卓越；卓越地位
77	at the heart of	在……的核心；是……的关键
78	merchant	商人；批发商
79	revolutionary	革命性的；创新的
80	ambitious	有雄心的；雄心勃勃的
81	bankroll	资助；提供资金给
82	ingeniousness	独创性；巧妙
83	inquisitive	好奇的；求知欲强的
84	singular	独特的；非凡的
85	incorporate into	合并；融入

	English	Chinese
86	shatter	粉碎;打碎
87	evade	逃避;回避
88	historian	历史学家;史学家
89	discovery	发现;探索
90	talent	才能;天赋
91	curiosity	好奇心;求知欲
92	seductive	诱人的;迷人的
93	imperialism	帝国主义;帝国主义制度
94	decline	下降;衰退
95	exchange	交流;交换
96	remarkable	卓越的;非凡的
97	draw up	起草;拟定
98	marvel at	对……感到惊奇;对……大为赞叹
99	intimately	紧密地;亲密地
100	achievement	成就;成绩

Word List 17

	English	Chinese
1	distinct	有区别的;清楚的
2	square	使平正;挺直(肩、腰等)
3	discreetly	谨慎地;小心地
4	clutch	紧抓；(因害怕或痛苦)突然抓住
5	glimpse	瞥见;开始理解
6	reserve	内向;矜持;寡言少语
7	whereabouts	下落;去向

	English	Chinese
8	demeanor	风度;举止;行为
9	scribble	潦草地写
10	grope for	探索
11	tip off	(向某人)密报,举报
12	goody	好吃的东西
13	flail	乱动;胡乱摆动
14	maneuver	策略;军事演习
15	rear end	臀部;后部
16	ketchup	番茄酱
17	sandal	凉鞋
18	brigade	一伙人;一帮人
19	sneak	潜行;偷拿
20	crunchy	松脆的
21	junk food	垃圾食品
22	tiptoe	踮着脚走;蹑手蹑脚地走
23	poor soul	可怜的人
24	spaghetti	意大利式细面条
25	go out to	同情某人
26	clasp	紧握;紧抱
27	grin	露齿而笑;咧着嘴笑
28	slink	溜;偷偷摸摸地走
29	malicious	怀有恶意的;恶毒的
30	run with the crowd	随波逐流
31	preoccupation	全神贯注;心事重重
32	shackle	束缚;羁绊;枷锁
33	puddle	水洼;小水坑
34	pose	姿势;装腔作势

	English	Chinese
35	humiliate	羞辱;使蒙羞
36	live up to	不辜负（他人的期望）
37	law of survival	生存法则
38	deliberation	考虑;审慎
39	assure	使确信;确保
40	distress	使悲伤;使忧虑
41	break into	闯入;破门而入
42	break out	爆发;突发
43	die down	逐渐变弱;逐渐平息
44	assume	假定;假设
45	relaxation	消遣;娱乐活动
46	familiarity	通晓;亲近
47	strategy	策略;战略
48	assortment	各式各样;混合
49	interpretation	解释;演绎
50	immaturity	未成熟;幼稚
51	stretch	伸展;延伸
52	galaxy	星系
53	spasm	迸发
54	organism	生物体
55	tectonic	地壳构造的
56	not least	尤其
57	tip	打翻
58	detriment	伤害
59	corrective	修改;纠正
60	hospitable	热情友好的
61	unprecedented	史无前例的

	English	Chinese
62	cultivation	耕种
63	conceit	自负
64	be coupled with	与……结合
65	ignorance	忽视
66	crash	猛撞；坠毁
67	gloomy	悲伤的
68	prediction	预测
69	arise from	摆脱贫困、不幸等
70	inventiveness	创造才能
71	inadvertence	粗心大意
72	symbiosis	共生（关系）
73	push...to the edge	把……置于危险之中
74	degradation	退化
75	accumulation	累积
76	biodiversity	生物多样性
77	far from	远非；完全不
78	remedy	解决良方；改进办法
79	publicity	宣传；推广
80	apart from	除了
81	diminish	减少
82	conundrum	复杂难题
83	immodest	自负的
84	cope with	解决
85	fundamental	基本规律；根本法则
86	ozone	臭氧
87	primacy	首要
88	exploitation	开采

	English	**Chinese**
89	consumption	消耗
90	uncommonly	罕见地
91	plausibility	貌似有理
92	bring in	引进
93	subsidiary	隶属的
94	environment	环境
95	ice age	冰河世纪
96	ecosystem	生态系统
97	atmosphere	大气；环境
98	acidification	酸化
99	superb	极好的
100	replace	取代

Word List 18

	English	**Chinese**
1	not... any more than...	与……同样不……
2	none other than	竟然
3	at a glance	一瞥；立刻
4	assurance	保证；信心
5	reassurance	安慰；保证
6	confidently	自信地；有把握地
7	confidentially	秘密地；私下地
8	lure into	诱骗……进入（某处）或做（某事）
9	consciousness	知觉；意识
10	conscientiousness	认真；勤勉

	English	Chinese
11	vacant	空着的；(职位、工作)空缺的
12	distinct from	区别于
13	dominate	支配；在……中占首要地位
14	to mechanically memorize	死记硬背
15	definite	清晰的；肯定的
16	obituary	讣闻；讣告
17	coronary	冠状的；花冠的
18	workaholic	工作狂
19	conceivably	可能地；可以想象地
20	discreetly	谨慎地；小心地
21	executive	行政的；经理的
22	execution	实施；处决
23	extracurricular	课外的
24	survive	幸存；比……活得久
25	stay up	熬夜
26	board	(在学校)寄宿
27	widow	寡妇；遗孀
28	deceased	死者；已故者
29	look sb. in the eye	直视某人；正视某人
30	straighten out	清理；整理
31	lineup	(准备参加某一活动的)一组人，阵容
32	grab	抓住；抓取
33	replace	把……放回原处
34	pick out	精心挑选
35	classic	经典作品；杰作
36	marketable	畅销的；有销路的
37	precise	准确的；确切的

	English	Chinese
38	competitiveness	竞争力;竞争性
39	sarcastic	讽刺的;挖苦的
40	die of	死于
41	care for	照顾;喜欢
42	acquaintance	泛泛之交;熟人
43	vice-president	副总裁;副总统
44	retire	退休;退役
45	survivor	幸存者;生还者
46	manufacturing	制造业
47	funeral	葬礼;丧礼
48	embarrassed	尴尬的;拮据的
49	bitterness	苦味;怨恨
50	inquiry	询问;调查
51	crowd out	挤出;排挤出
52	stench	恶臭
53	manipulation	操纵
54	degradation	衰退
55	ethical	伦理的
56	accustomed	习惯的
57	plainly	明白地
58	application	应用
59	open up	打开;开辟
60	debasement	贬低;贬值
61	moral	道德的
62	specter	恐惧;恐慌
63	in effect	实际上
64	destruction	破坏

	English	Chinese
65	suffice	足够
66	remedy	补救;改正
67	have the grounds for	有理由
68	utopia	乌托邦
69	evil	有害的
70	hand-wringer	坐立不安的人
71	draw on	利用
72	catch up	赶上
73	inherently	内在地;固有地
74	misunderstanding	误解
75	supersede	代替
76	undreamt of	做梦都没想到的
77	allegiance	忠诚
78	remake	重做;改编
79	neutral	中立的
80	feed off	以……为食
81	beware of	当心;提防
82	impotent	无能为力的
83	flatten	使变平
84	lie in	在于
85	dominate	支配
86	debate	辩论
87	in light of	由于
88	ascendancy	优势
89	assumption	(责任的)承担
90	progressive	渐进的
91	dystopia	反乌托邦

	English	Chinese
92	refine	改善
93	allude to	暗指；影射
94	evolve	进化
95	replace	更换；更新
96	cumulatively	累积地
97	an array of	一批
98	ambiguous	模棱两可的
99	philosophy	哲学
100	religion	宗教

Word List 19

	English	Chinese
1	unsought	未经请求的；主动提供的
2	disorientated	不知所措的；迷失方向的
3	be versed in	精通
4	grossly	很；非常
5	astound	使惊骇；使震惊
6	thrust	猛推；戳
7	comradeship	友好情谊；同志关系
8	down-to-earth	务实的；切合实际的
9	accomplished	熟练的；才华高的
10	rotten	腐烂的；腐败的
11	squalid	肮脏的；不道德的
12	pound	连续重击；(心脏)狂跳
13	middle ground	中间立场

	English	Chinese
14	verse	诗;韵文
15	bard	诗人;游吟诗人
16	imponderable	无法衡量的;难以断定的
17	evolve	(使)逐渐形成
18	veritable	真正的;名副其实的
19	elevate	提拔;提高
20	mediocre	平庸的;中等(质量)的
21	lyric	歌词;抒情诗
22	epic	史诗
23	rule of thumb	经验常识工作法
24	conjure up	想起;使在脑海中显现
25	cuddle	搂抱;拥抱
26	aroma	芳香;香味
27	prosaic	平庸的;乏味的
28	aura	气氛;氛围
29	break the ice	打破沉默;使气氛活跃
30	incidentally	顺便提一句;附带地
31	inquire into	调查
32	inquire as to	询问;打听
33	inquire after	问候;询问(健康状况)
34	inquire about	询问;打听
35	at odds	意见不一致;不和
36	irreplaceable	不可替代的
37	irremediable	不能弥补的;无法医治的
38	conceive of	想象;设想
39	deceive	欺骗;蒙骗
40	perceive	注意到;意识到

	English	Chinese
41	instantly	瞬间；立即
42	promptly	敏捷地
43	readily	便利地；欣然地
44	make the acquaintance of sb.	结识某人
45	gain on	（比赛中）接近
46	nail down	敲定；确定
47	rule out	排除；取消
48	get across	被传达；被理解
49	go after	追求；追逐
50	reflect on	深思；考虑
51	neighboring	邻近的
52	repackage	重新包装
53	diverse	不同的
54	flood into	涌入
55	open-mindedness	心胸开阔
56	triumphant	大获全胜的
57	rambling	规划凌乱的
58	profess	宣称
59	unfathomably	难以理解地
60	slope	斜坡
61	cut-throat	残酷的
62	standard-issue	标准的
63	rechannel	使改道
64	tree-lined	（街道等）树木成排的
65	excel in	擅长
66	nippy	寒冷的
67	ramp up	增加

	English	Chinese
68	drop out	退学
69	commute	通勤
70	willowy	苗条的
71	psychiatry	精神病学
72	flicker	闪烁
73	licensed	得到许可的
74	enroll in	参加
75	overqualified	资历过高的
76	discipline	纪律
77	scamper	蹦蹦跳跳
78	tight-knit	紧密团结的
79	envision	展望；想象
80	pride oneself on	以……自豪
81	corporal punishment	体罚
82	transcript	（根据录音的）文字记录
83	thrum	持续嗡嗡声
84	chew over	仔细考虑
85	emulate	模仿
86	boarding school	寄宿学校
87	profile	印象；形象
88	low-keyness	低调
89	buoy up	使浮起
90	globetrotting	周游世界的
91	get sth. off the ground	开始
92	in the throes of	处于……困境（或痛苦）中
93	take apart	拆开
94	pay lip service to	口惠而实不至

	English	Chinese
95	long-term	长期的
96	enlist	招募
97	less-than-rewarding	得不偿失的
98	all-encompassing	包罗万象的
99	working-class	工人阶级的
100	aversion	厌恶

Word List 20

	English	Chinese
1	transaction	交易;业务
2	avocation	业余爱好
3	panel	专家咨询组;专题讨论小组
4	glamorous	富有魅力的
5	bohemian	放荡不羁的;波希米亚的
6	arduous	辛勤的;艰巨的
7	go broke	破产;身无分文
8	circulate	(尤指在聚会上)往来应酬
9	solitary	独自的;孤单的
10	drudge	单调乏味的工作;苦工
11	symbolism	象征主义;符号体系
12	mime	哑剧表演;哑剧
13	gusto	热情高涨;兴致勃勃
14	revelation	披露;揭露
15	bewildered	糊涂的;困惑的
16	fiddle with	不停地摆弄（或拨弄）

	English	Chinese
17	compulsion	强制;强迫
18	gimmick	吸引人的花招;噱头
19	clutter	杂乱的东西;杂物
20	chic	时髦的;优雅的
21	draw into	使卷入;使参与
22	stick to	坚持;维持
23	bring along	带来;培养
24	ponder	沉思;琢磨
25	conceive	构思;设想
26	reckon	想;认为
27	conflict	冲突;争执
28	contradiction	矛盾;不一致
29	confrontation	对峙;冲突
30	entail	牵涉;需要
31	restore to	恢复;归还
32	insanity	精神错乱;荒唐的行为
33	disposition	性格;倾向
34	insight	洞悉;洞察力
35	collision	碰撞;互撞
36	combat	搏斗;打仗
37	secure	(尤指经过努力而)获得
38	claim	索赔
39	exclaim	呼喊;惊叫
40	reclaim	取回;要求归还
41	acclaim	赞扬;称赞
42	afflict	折磨;使痛苦
43	afflictive	使人痛苦的;折磨人的

	English	Chinese
44	inflict	使吃苦头；使遭受打击
45	adverse	不利的；有害的
46	converse	相反的
47	reverse	相反的；反向的
48	let it all hang out	轻松随便；不拘礼节
49	occur to	被想到；出现在头脑中
50	commit an act of sth.	做某事
51	dismal	忧郁的；凄凉的
52	wily	诡计多端的
53	at a clip of	以……的速度
54	prosperity	繁荣
55	covet	觊觎
56	toil	苦活
57	notch up	完成
58	wellness	健康
59	espouse	支持
60	necessity	必需品
61	better off	较富裕的
62	upstart	自命不凡的
63	cater to	迎合；满足
64	by necessity	必然地
65	paradox	似是而非的矛盾说法
66	adherent	拥护者
67	derive from	源于
68	folksy	友好的
69	defer to	听从；遵从
70	affluent	富裕的

	English	Chinese
71	ossify	使僵化
72	be adept at	擅长
73	luxury	奢侈品
74	budge	(使)移动;推动
75	draw on	利用
76	take for granted	认为……理所当然
77	frill	(衣服、窗帘等的)饰边
78	from afar	从远处
79	in search of	寻找
80	become inured to	习惯于
81	take sth. downmarket	把某物降低档次
82	capitalism	资本主义
83	cast doubt on	怀疑
84	aspire	渴望;向往
85	well-being	幸福;健康
86	rat race	(为金钱、权力、地位等的)疯狂竞争
87	hierarchy	等级制度
88	pecking order	权势等级;啄序
89	venerate	敬重;崇敬
90	keep up	跟上
91	frivolous	无关紧要的
92	busy oneself doing sth.	使忙于
93	materialism	实利主义;物质主义
94	niche	商机
95	stagnation	停滞
96	do the trick	奏效;起作用
97	flip side	反面;负面

	English	Chinese
98	idyllic	田园诗般的
99	look down on	看不起
100	assiduous	刻苦的

Word List 21

	English	Chinese
1	entertain	心存,怀有(想法、希望、感觉等)
2	yearn	渴望;渴求
3	attain	(通常指经过努力)获得,得到
4	be indicative of	指示;表明
5	revealing	揭露真相的;发人深省的
6	confirm	确证;证实
7	involve	包含;牵涉
8	comprise	由……组成
9	effect	影响;结果
10	feeble	虚弱的;无力的
11	literate	有读写能力的
12	literacy	读写能力
13	literal	字面意思的;完全按原文的
14	be lacking in	缺乏
15	stick at sth.	坚持不懈;锲而不舍
16	stick into sth.	插入;戳入
17	stick up for sb./sth.	支持;捍卫
18	of the essence	绝对必要的;不可或缺的
19	stern	船尾

	English	Chinese
20	quarter	城镇的区（或一部分）
21	close quarters	近距离
22	guts	（尤指动物的）内脏
23	doze off	（尤指在日间）打瞌睡
24	canteen	（士兵、旅游者等用的）水壶
25	crave	渴望；恳求
26	sunken	沉没的；凹陷的
27	swell	海浪的涌动；涌浪
28	scorch	烧焦；枯萎
29	clog	阻塞；堵塞
30	sprawl	伸开四肢坐（或躺）；蔓延
31	gunwale	船舷上缘，舷缘
32	taunt	嘲讽；奚落
33	ration	定量供应；实行配给
34	keel over	突然倒下；晕倒
35	paralysis	麻痹；瘫痪
36	vague	不明确的；不清楚的
37	yield	屈服；让步
38	prop up	支撑；撑起（某物）
39	adrift	漫无目的的；茫然的
40	stare	凝视；盯着看
41	mirage	海市蜃楼；幻想
42	growl	咆哮；发低沉的怒吼
43	heft	举起；掂……的重量
44	take over	取代；占上风
45	sleep away	睡觉打发时间；睡觉消除（烦恼等）
46	hold out	坚持；维持

	English	Chinese
47	hold off	观望；拖延
48	give in	屈服；认输
49	grim	严肃的；坚定的
50	calculating	精明的；精于算计的
51	opponent	反对者
52	partial	部分的
53	combat	战斗
54	disposable	一次性的
55	attribute to	把……归因于
56	payroll	工资名单
57	betrayal	背叛
58	netherworld	底层社会
59	minimum wage	（法定的）最低工资
60	viable	切实可行的
61	incarnation	（生活中的）特殊阶段
62	stagnation	停滞
63	hostility	敌意
64	onerous	费力的；艰巨的
65	in particular	尤其
66	enshrine	把……奉为神圣
67	take over	接管
68	humiliation	耻辱
69	disincentive	阻碍因素；遏制因素
70	cope with	处理
71	robust	强健的；强壮的
72	labor union	工会
73	revoke	撤销

	English	Chinese
74	stem from	起源于
75	in the realm of	在……领域里
76	deadlock	僵局
77	pervasive	遍布的
78	beget	产生；引起
79	advocate	拥护者
80	at the disposal of	任……支配
81	surrender to	投降；屈服
82	reinforce	加强
83	hypertrophy	过度增大
84	civil servant	公务员
85	precariousness	不稳固；不牢靠
86	inflexible	不灵活的
87	at the expense of	以……为代价
88	humane	人道的
89	defend the status quo	维持现状
90	collective bargaining	(劳资双方就工资和工作条件进行的)集体谈判
91	withdraw	撤回
92	multiply	成倍增加
93	exacerbate	使恶化
94	be grounded in	以……为基础
95	lament	悲叹
96	in the name of	以……的名义
97	cling to	坚持
98	welfare state	福利国家
99	labor code	劳动法
100	protest	抗议

Word List 22

	English	Chinese
1	volunteer	自愿做；义务做
2	profess to	妄称；伪称
3	earth-shattering	惊天动地的；极其重大的
4	feign	假装；装作
5	spare one's feelings	照顾某人的感受
6	preoccupation	使人全神贯注的事物
7	prevarication	搪塞；支吾
8	devote to	致力于
9	serial	连续的；多次的
10	profession	（需要掌握专门的知识或技能的）职业
11	pundit	专家；权威
12	consultant	顾问；会诊医师
13	shape or spin the truth	编造或歪曲事实
14	client	客户；委托人
15	ubiquitous	普遍存在的；无所不在的
16	fib	无伤大雅的谎言；小谎
17	invariably	始终如一地；一贯地
18	blurt out	脱口而出
19	deceit	欺骗；欺诈
20	compliment sb. on sth.	因某事称赞某人
21	lubricant	润滑剂；润滑油
22	tangled	缠结的；复杂的
23	entangle	使纠缠；使卷入
24	wear down	磨损；使精疲力竭

	English	Chinese
25	distinction	差别;区别
26	perception	看法;洞察力
27	warp	使变形;使反常
28	think highly of	高度评价;尊重
29	proliferation	增殖
30	cynicism	愤世嫉俗;冷嘲热讽
31	cynical	愤世嫉俗的;悲观的,怀疑的;损人利己的
32	falter	衰弱;蹒跚
33	be avoided at all costs	不惜一切代价以避免
34	associate	同事;副职
35	undermine	暗中破坏
36	rule of thumb	经验法则
37	confound	使困惑惊讶;使惊疑
38	amaze	使惊奇;使惊愕
39	unethical	不道德的
40	preoccupy	使全神贯注;困扰
41	unsparing	严厉的;不吝惜的
42	willful	任性的;故意的
43	gaze	凝视;注视
44	gape	张口;目瞪口呆
45	stare	凝视;注视
46	glare	怒目而视
47	grumble	嘟囔;发牢骚
48	by instinct	出于本能;出于天性
49	on instinct	凭直觉
50	brute	粗野的人;残忍的人
51	comprise	包括

	English	Chinese
52	merge with	融入
53	venture	冒险
54	confine to	限于
55	underestimate	低估
56	delicate	脆弱的
57	initiate	创始;发起
58	for good	永久地
59	encounter	偶遇
60	savagery	残暴行为
61	studio	工作室;画室
62	influential	有影响力的
63	intermediary	中间人
64	defend	捍卫
65	coincide with	巧合
66	correspondence	信件
67	owe to	归功于
68	print	版画
69	at length	详尽地
70	conceal	隐藏;藏匿
71	put one's foot down	坚持立场
72	pile up	堆积
73	distorted	扭曲的
74	budge	让步
75	degenerate	堕落的
76	aggressiveness	攻击性
77	manipulate	操纵;控制
78	subversive	颠覆性的

	English	Chinese
79	portrait	肖像
80	spare	备件；备用品
81	discouraging	使人沮丧的
82	disconcerting	令人惊慌失措的
83	legitimacy	合法性
84	deconstruction	解构
85	superlative	(形容词或副词的)最高级
86	ambitious	有抱负的
87	upheaval	剧变
88	dispute	争论
89	reception	反响
90	baffled	困惑的
91	masterstroke	绝招；高招
92	exclusive	独有的
93	at the request of	应……的邀请
94	conceivably	可想象地
95	envision	想象
96	span	持续；贯穿
97	serenity	平静
98	long-standing	长期存在的
99	highlight	强调
100	burn bridges with	与……中断联系

Word List

	English	Chinese
1	creaky	嘎吱作响的；破旧的

	English	Chinese
2	peer	仔细看;端详
3	buff	浅黄褐色
4	make sb.'s acquaintance	结识某人
5	laxative	泻药
6	perceive	理解;领会
7	perceptible	可察觉到的;看得出的
8	imperceptible	无法觉察的;察觉不到的
9	autopsy	验尸;尸体剖检
10	apprehensively	担心地
11	potion	饮剂;药水
12	oblige	(按法律或规则)强迫,强制
13	disoblige	得罪;冒犯
14	indulge in	沉溺于
15	confidential	机密的;保密的
16	bountifully	慷慨地;丰富地
17	substitute	代替;替换
18	scorn	蔑视;轻视
19	giddy	轻浮的;令人眩晕的
20	rapture	兴高采烈
21	rapt	全神贯注的
22	sole	唯一的;仅有的
23	draught	穿堂风;通风气流
24	overwhelm	压垮;使应接不暇
25	fervently	热切地;热烈地
26	phial	小药瓶;管形瓶
27	be better off	有较多钱;比较宽裕
28	reach for	伸手去拿

	English	Chinese
29	obscure	晦涩的;费解的
30	obscurity	无名;默默无闻
31	save up	储蓄;贮存
32	deal in	经营;交易
33	permanent	永久的;永恒的
34	detachment	客观;冷漠
35	indicative	指示的;象征的
36	revealing	揭露真相的;发人深省的
37	shiver	(因寒冷或害怕而)哆嗦,发抖
38	intense	十分强烈的;激烈的
39	intensive	彻底的;十分细致的
40	unalterably	不可改变地;坚定不移地
41	invariable	始终如一的;永无变化的
42	consequently	因此;所以
43	consistently	一贯地;一致地
44	compliment	赞扬;问候
45	complement	补充;补足
46	aftermath	(战争、风暴、事故的)后果,余波
47	involvement	参与;投入
48	intrinsic	内在的;固有的
49	in consequence	因此;结果
50	in consequence of	由于;作为……的结果
51	explosion	爆发
52	sought after	受欢迎的
53	crisply	酥脆地
54	credit	声望;荣誉
55	pitch	投;掷

	English	Chinese
56	picky	挑剔的
57	stratagem	策略；计策
58	nuisance	麻烦事；讨厌的人（或事物、情况）
59	not least	明显地
60	cutting edge	尖端；前沿
61	hasten	促进
62	circulation	流通
63	profit from	得益于
64	measurable	显著的
65	forecast	预测
66	well-worn	陈词滥调的
67	specialize in	专攻
68	proportion	比例
69	trumpet	宣扬；吹捧
70	consultancy	咨询服务
71	gossip	流言蜚语
72	dominate	支配
73	spin	具有倾向性的陈述
74	drum up	竭力争取（支持）
75	oust	驱逐
76	console	控制台；仪表板
77	flawed	有缺陷的
78	have one's say	有发言权
79	serve up	给出；提供
80	huff	生气地说；怒气冲冲地说
81	fragmentation	分裂
82	suppress	抑制

	English	Chinese
83	proliferation	激增
84	mediate	调停
85	in-house	(机构)内部的
86	puff	吹捧
87	commentator	评论员
88	have an appetite for	对……感兴趣
89	sceptic	持怀疑态度的人
90	hard-core	中坚的;骨干的
91	accentuate	强调
92	airing	晾晒;透风
93	triumphalism	耀武扬威
94	boost	助推
95	entitle	给予权利
96	purveyor	提供者
97	consolidate	加强;巩固
98	desperate for	渴望
99	buzz	轰动效应
100	peer group	同辈群体

Word List

	English	Chinese
1	venerable	(因年岁、品格、地位等)值得尊敬的
2	leafy	多叶的;多树木的
3	residential	居民区的
4	agreeable	愉悦的

	English	Chinese
5	virtually	事实上
6	debonair	（男人）温文尔雅的,潇洒的
7	eccentric	古怪的
8	curb	马路牙子
9	reluctant	勉强的
10	depart	出发
11	guiltily	内疚地
12	sedate	宁静的
13	compact	紧凑的
14	habituate	使习惯于
15	unfurl	打开;展开
16	contortion	扭曲的动作
17	ludicrous	不合理的
18	extravagant	过度的
19	squash	壁球
20	undertaking	（重大或艰巨的）任务,工程
21	treadmill	跑步机
22	calorie	卡路里
23	concerned	关心的
24	faintly	微弱地
25	horrified	令人震惊的;令人惊恐的
26	budget	规划;安排
27	facility	设施
28	pedestrian	行人
29	sidewalk	人行道
30	dodge	躲开
31	lane	车道

	English	Chinese
32	swiftly	很快地
33	ridiculous	荒谬的
34	exasperating	使人恼怒的
35	notion	想法；观念
36	entertain	怀有（想法、希望、感觉等）
37	negotiate	通过，越过（险要路段）
38	intersection	十字路口；交叉路口
39	woe	麻烦
40	comprehensive	全面的
41	renewal	恢复
42	esthetically	在审美方面
43	coo	（尤指对所爱的人）轻柔低语
44	anew	重新；再
45	thrive	繁荣
46	tub	盆；桶
47	pull up	停止
48	go about	开始做；着手做
49	pedestrian crossing	人行横道
50	bring sth. home to sb.	使某人了解某事的重要性（或艰难、严重程度）
51	despise	厌恶
52	condemn	谴责
53	materialism	物质主义；唯物主义
54	at best	充其量
55	vice and virtue	善恶
56	profiteer	牟取暴利者
57	rogue	流氓
58	conceal	遮盖；遮住

	English	Chinese
59	deceive	使人误信;误导
60	adept	能手;内行
61	confer on	授予
62	notoriously	臭名昭著地
63	oppressive	压迫的
64	burgeoning	迅速发展的
65	manifestation	显示
66	authorial	作者的
67	in view of	鉴于
68	abode	住所
69	degradation	侮辱;贬低
70	graft	贪污
71	unrestrained	放纵的
72	outstrip	超过
73	scornful	轻蔑的
74	contempt	蔑视
75	persist	坚持
76	idiosyncratic	独特的
77	nexus	联系
78	abyss	深渊
79	overspan	跨越
80	verily	真正地;真实地
81	compel	强迫
82	take account of	考虑到
83	animosity	敌意
84	inflict	施加
85	cut-throat	激烈竞争的

	English	Chinese
86	predecessor	前任
87	syndrome	综合征
88	denigration	诽谤；贬低
89	ruthless	无情的
90	go-getter	有进取心的人
91	entrap	诱捕
92	measure up to	符合；达到
93	cynicism	愤世嫉俗
94	bearing	举止
95	unprecedented	空前的
96	outrage	愤怒
97	sinister	邪恶的
98	successor	继任者
99	foremost	最重要的；最著名的
100	superiority	优势

Word List 25

	English	Chinese
1	catastrophic	灾难性的；极糟的
2	misfortune	厄运；灾难
3	ups and downs	浮沉；兴衰
4	desperately	绝望地；拼命地
5	unmeasured	无边无际的；无限的
6	menace	威胁；烦人的人
7	lull	间歇；平静期

	English	Chinese
8	deceptive	欺骗性的
9	deception	欺骗
10	deceit	骗术;诡计
11	deceive	对……不忠
12	triumph	(成功的)典范,楷模
13	impostor	骗子;冒充者
14	basically	大体上;基本上
15	petty	无足轻重的
16	conviction	判罪;定罪
17	yield to	屈服;让步
18	overwhelming	(感情)极强烈的
19	might	力量;威力
20	liquidate	变卖;变现
21	sponge	(用海绵)清洗,擦拭
22	slate	板岩;石板
23	flinch	退缩;畏惧
24	persevere	坚持;孜孜以求
25	compliment	赞美;恭维
26	venture	小心地说;谨慎地做
27	stern	严厉的;严峻的
28	station	岗位;职位
29	cast one's mind back	使人想起
30	eyewitness account	目击者的描述
31	give in	让步;勉强同意
32	go through	(法律、合同等正式)通过
33	in the position	处在……位置上;担任
34	address oneself to	致力于

	English	Chinese
35	stand in the gap	挺身阻挡;首当其冲
36	in sb.'s honour	向……表示敬意
37	contaminate	污染;弄脏
38	contemplate	考虑;思量
39	enforcement	执行;实施
40	reinforcement	援兵;增援部队
41	specifically	特意;专门地
42	noble	高尚的;崇高的
43	eminent	(在某领域或职业中)卓越的,出众的
44	supplement	增补(物);补充(物)
45	implement	贯彻;执行
46	business depression	商业萧条
47	impose	迫使;把……强加于
48	impair	损害;削弱
49	coercion	强迫;胁迫
50	complimentary	赞美的;免费的
51	mainstream media	主流媒体
52	mass media	大众传媒
53	elite media	精英媒体
54	play up	彰显;夸大
55	scholarship	奖学金
56	constraint	限制
57	radically	根本上
58	go up and back	来来回回
59	molecule	分子
60	hypothesis	假设
61	conform to	符合

	English	Chinese
62	virtually	事实上
63	assumption	就职;任职
64	overwhelming	令人不知所措的
65	agenda	议题
66	privileged	享有特权的
67	in (a)…fashion	以……方式
68	executive	主管;经理
69	framework	框架
70	grind out	大量生产(常指粗制滥造)
71	divert	娱乐;供消遣
72	off line	不在工作(或运行)
73	power play	高压攻势
74	break the mold	打破常规
75	run the show	操纵局势
76	outright	完全的
77	tyrannical	专横的
78	hierarchic	等级制度的
79	doctrinal	教义的
80	scatter	撒播
81	parasitic	寄生的
82	grant	(政府、机构的)拨款
83	internalize	使内在化
84	weed out	清除
85	filter	过滤
86	a pain in the neck	极讨厌的人(或事物)
87	gear to	使适合
88	conformity	遵照;顺从

	English	Chinese
89	obedience	服从
90	end up	最终成为；最后处于
91	troublemaker	捣乱者
92	upscale	高端的
93	null hypothesis	（统计测试中的）零假设，虚假设
94	conjecture	猜想
95	slanted	有倾向性的
96	pragmatic	务实的
97	saturation	饱和
98	put great demands on	大量占用
99	foster good relations with	建立良好的关系
100	off the record	私下的；不得发表的

Word List

	English	Chinese
1	assessment	评价；估计
2	extract	摘录；提取物
3	thoughtful	体贴入微的；考虑周到的
4	proficient	熟练的；精通的
5	sufficient	足够的；充足的
6	efficient	效率高的
7	assemble	聚集；装配
8	simulate	模拟；模仿
9	accumulate	积累；积攒
10	forge	缔造；伪造

	English	Chinese
11	for the better	好转
12	take advantage of	利用
13	be available for	可供……之用
14	give ... pause	踌躇
15	be confronted with	面对
16	in earnest	认真地；严肃地
17	at the expense of	以……为代价
18	be given to	沉溺于；癖好
19	prior to	在……之前
20	have access to	能接近、接触或使用
21	depressed	抑郁的；沮丧的
22	foster	促进；培养
23	simulated	模拟的；模仿的
24	cyberspace	网络空间
25	surf	上网；冲浪
26	perceive	把……看作；认为
27	converse	相反的事物；反面说法
28	gratification	满足；令人喜悦的事物
29	oyster	牡蛎；蚝
30	at the very least	至少；起码
31	alienation	疏远；离间
32	addicted	上瘾的；入迷的
33	alcoholic	酒精的；含酒精的
34	moderate	中等的；不偏激的
35	temperate	温和的；自我克制的
36	adequate	足够的；合格的
37	intricate	错综复杂的

	English	Chinese
38	exaggeration	夸张;言过其实
39	binge	大吃大喝
40	skew	歪曲;偏离
41	forum	论坛;讨论会
42	access	通道;途径
43	modal	情态的;形式的
44	potential	可能性;潜在机会
45	dramatically	戏剧性地;夸张地
46	fragmentation	破碎,分裂;分段储存
47	fragment	碎裂;分裂
48	fragmentary	残缺不全的;不完整的
49	alienate	使疏远;使不友好
50	acquaint	使熟悉;使了解
51	seduction	诱惑
52	pioneer	先驱
53	fantasy	幻想
54	peddle	兜售;宣传
55	metamorphosis	变形;质变
56	skeptic	怀疑（论）者
57	unconventional	非常规的
58	harbor	怀有
59	messianic	救世主的
60	faith	信念
61	hostility	敌意
62	revival	复兴
63	on everyone's lips	大家都在讨论的
64	democratize	民主化
65	reverent	恭敬的

	English	Chinese
66	amateur	业余爱好者
67	seasick	晕船的
68	at the heart of	位于……的中心
69	fall on deaf ears	未被理睬
70	cacophony	刺耳的声音
71	sneak	偷偷地走
72	beta version	测试版
73	anarchy	无政府状态
74	infinite	无限的
75	opinionated	固执己见的
76	prevail	获胜；占优势
77	filibustering	（议会中为拖延表决的）冗长演说
78	narcissism	自恋
79	swell	膨胀；肿胀
80	dismay	使诧异；使惊愕
81	undermine	在……下挖
82	belittle	贬低
83	spawn	造成；产生
84	purveyor	提供者
85	plagiarism	剽窃
86	stifle	抑制
87	disguise	伪装
88	anonymous	匿名的
89	hijack	劫持
90	preach	鼓吹
91	perpetuate	使永久
92	masquerade	掩藏；掩饰

	English	Chinese
93	whipping boy	替罪羊
94	consensus	共识
95	violation	违反
96	patent	专利
97	confession	承认
98	untrustworthy	不可靠的
99	absurd	荒谬的
100	inanity	浅薄;愚蠢

Word List

	English	Chinese
1	dispatch	派遣;发送（邮件、包裹、信息）
2	constitute	（被认为或看作）是;被算作
3	artistry	艺术技巧
4	char	（把……）烧焦,烧黑
5	pulse	脉搏;(声波或光波的)脉冲
6	ledge	壁架;横档
7	unearthly	怪异的;异常的
8	rubble	碎石;碎砖
9	brand with	打烙印于;以烙铁打（标记）
10	for keeps	永久地;永远地
11	witness	目睹（某事发生）
12	stumble	绊脚;绊倒
13	outskirts	市郊;郊区
14	ruin	毁坏;破坏

	English	Chinese
15	hang over	逼近;威胁
16	spare	宽恕;饶恕
17	intact	完好无损的
18	glimpse	瞥见;开始理解
19	apprehend	逮捕;拘捕
20	peril	巨大的危险;危难
21	counterpoise	均衡;补偿
22	dispel	驱散,消除（尤指感觉或信仰）
23	continuation	连续;持续
24	continuity	连续性;连贯性
25	ensure	确保;保证
26	come into existence	存在
27	in a flash	瞬间;立刻
28	once and for all	最后;彻底地
29	in certain respects	在某些方面
30	lie in	（问题、事情等）在于
31	come into one's own	显出自己的本事
32	universal	普遍的;全世界的
33	in the shadow of	处在……的阴影中
34	enroll	注册;招（生）
35	subscribe	订阅
36	swerve	突然改变方向,急转弯
37	contort	扭曲;歪曲
38	expanse	（陆地、水面或天空的）广阔区域
39	stretch	伸出;伸长;拉伸
40	collide with	与……相撞
41	coincide with	与……一致

	English	Chinese
42	stumble on	意外发现;偶然遇见
43	tumble on	恍然大悟;顿悟
44	disqualify	使不合格;使不合适
45	disfavor	不赞成
46	verify	核实;核查
47	assume	假装;装出
48	presume	假设;假定
49	attain	(通过努力)获得
50	principal	最重要的;主要的
51	prejudice	损害;有损于
52	prevail	流行;盛行
53	cock	歪戴(帽子)
54	saunter	闲逛
55	sot	醉鬼
56	appellation	称号
57	glutton	贪吃的人
58	exert	运用
59	despisingly	鄙视地;蔑视地
60	assume an air of	装出……的样子
61	frugal	节俭的
62	petty	器量小的
63	affected	做作的
64	muse on	沉思
65	ratify	正式批准
66	patriotism	爱国主义
67	peremptory	专横的
68	judicious	明智的
69	approbation	认可

	English	Chinese
70	take occasion to	抓住机会
71	sycophant	谄媚者
72	dispute	争论
73	attend to	处理
74	deprive...of...	剥夺
75	multiplicity	多样性
76	not scruple to do	肆无忌惮地做
77	venture	(有风险的)经营活动,项目
78	forfeit	(因犯错)丧失
79	excel	擅长
80	avaricious	贪婪的
81	impetuous	鲁莽的
82	despond	沮丧
83	inveterate	根深蒂固的
84	be obliged to	被迫做
85	call into question	使人怀疑
86	ramble	漫步
87	stereotype	刻板印象
88	discrimination	歧视
89	infinite	极大的
90	refer to	查阅;参考
91	exemption from	豁免
92	benevolent	仁慈的
93	flattering	奉承的
94	make bold to do	冒昧做
95	boast of	炫耀;吹嘘
96	gravity	严肃

	English	Chinese
97	undaunted	勇敢的
98	contemplative	深思熟虑的
99	poltroon	懦夫
100	clemency	仁慈

Word List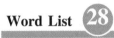

	English	Chinese
1	regulation	规定要求的;常规的
2	prompt	引起;导致;激起
3	expatriate	移居国外的人;侨民
4	barbecue	户外烧烤
5	suppress	(武力)镇压;抑制
6	heritage	遗产;传统
7	inheritance	继承;遗产
8	legacy	(计算机系统或产品)已停产的
9	twinge	一阵刺痛;一阵剧痛
10	unease	焦虑;不安
11	lacuna	(尤指书或手稿中的)脱漏,空白
12	folly	愚蠢;愚蠢的行为(或念头等)
13	reenactment	(对事件的)再现,重现
14	skirmish	小冲突;小规模战斗
15	launch	发射;投射
16	bonnet	(有带子并盖住耳朵的)童帽;(尤指旧时的)女帽
17	goggle-eyed	(通常指因为惊奇而)瞪大眼睛的
18	make-believe	假装的;假想的

	English	Chinese
19	swell	增加;增多
20	pursue	追赶;追捕
21	enlightenment	启迪;开导
22	riposte	机敏地回答
23	resonate with	与……产生共鸣
24	sinister	邪恶的;不祥的
25	personify	是……的化身（或典型）
26	cliché	陈词滥调;老生常谈
27	backdrop	（事件的）背景
28	peer	（才能、学识等方面）相匹敌的人
29	fleeciness	似羊毛的特点
30	confront	遭遇;正视
31	jarring	不和谐的
32	be immersed in	沉浸于;沉迷于
33	matter	事情;事件
34	occasion	时刻;时候;场合
35	coincidence	巧合;巧事
36	claim	声称;主张
37	confess	坦白;供认
38	declare	宣布;声明
39	confirm	巩固;加强
40	indicative	标示的;表明的
41	revealing	揭露真相的;发人深省的
42	evident	显而易见的
43	available	可获得的;可用的
44	acceptable	令人满意的;可以接受的
45	advisable	明智的;可取的

	English	Chinese
46	applicable	适合的;适用的
47	hypocritical	伪善的;虚伪的
48	perilous	危险的;艰险的
49	desperate	铤而走险的
50	give access to	为……提供进入的条件
51	bundle	捆绑
52	stoke	煽动
53	full-blown	成熟的
54	element	要素;基本部分
55	be tantamount to	(坏的品质或影响)等同于
56	dock	被告席
57	backlash	(尤指对政治或社会事件的)强烈反对
58	monopoly	垄断
59	ruling	裁决
60	protocol	条约草案;议定书
61	lobbyist	说客
62	stake out	清楚地界定自认为属于自己的东西
63	be accused of	被指控
64	precedent	范例
65	rampage	狂暴行为
66	live with	忍受
67	expire	期满;失效
68	be comparable to	可与……相提并论
69	license	批准;许可
70	interoperate	兼容
71	embolden	鼓励;使有胆量
72	incentive	激励;刺激

	English	Chinese
73	dish up	上菜；提出（事实、论点等）
74	provision	条款
75	comply with	遵守
76	royalty	使用费；版税
77	barrier to entry	进入（市场的）壁垒
78	dominant	占支配地位的
79	potential	潜在的
80	draw to a close	结束
81	antitrust	反垄断的
82	sovereignty	主权
83	uphold	支持
84	bone of contention	争论的焦点
85	amount to	相当于
86	impose	强加于
87	takeover	接管
88	curb	抑制
89	abusive	辱骂的；咒骂的
90	lock-in	（将一家公司）捆绑（在另一家上）
91	deal a blow to	令……震惊
92	champion	支持
93	endorse	赞同
94	discourage	阻碍
95	intellectual property	知识产权
96	rebate	返款；折扣
97	a slap on the wrist	轻微的惩罚
98	be wary of	谨慎的
99	withhold	拒绝给
100	chill	惊吓；使恐惧

Word List 29

	English	Chinese
1	undersized	小于正常（或一般）的；矮小的
2	nerve	神经；勇气
3	agony	（精神或肉体的）极度痛苦
4	delusion	错觉；妄想
5	grandeur	壮丽；雄伟
6	conceit	自负；骄傲自大
7	in relation to	关于；有关
8	roll in	大量涌入；滚滚而来
9	exhausting	使人精疲力竭的；使人疲惫不堪的
10	conversationalist	健谈的人
11	tiresome	烦人的；令人厌烦的
12	mania	狂热；躁狂症
13	harangue	呵斥；大声谴责
14	volubility	健谈；流利
15	for the sake of	为了……的利益/缘故
16	vegetarianism	素食主义
17	pamphlet	小册子；手册
18	at sb.'s expense	由某人付费
19	out of sorts	身体不适的；不太开心的
20	rave	极力赞扬；热情谈论
21	suicidal	有自杀倾向的；有致命危险的
22	gloom	忧郁；昏暗
23	grief-stricken	极度悲伤的
24	callous	冷酷无情的；冷漠的

	English	Chinese
25	shudder	(因恐惧、寒冷等)发抖,打战
26	be innocent of	无辜的;无罪的
27	by the score	大批;大量
28	grovel	匍匐;卑躬屈膝
29	loftily	高尚地;傲慢地
30	benefactor	捐助人;赞助人
31	recipient	受方;接受者
32	lay hands on	攫取;得到
33	unscrupulous	不诚实的;不公正的
34	procession	(人或车辆的)行列;一连串的人(或物)
35	infidelity	无宗教信仰;不信奉宗教
36	pull wires	幕后操纵
37	idiotic	十分愚蠢的;白痴般的
38	arrogance	傲慢;自大
39	caricature	人物漫画;夸张的描述
40	be content with	对……心满意足
41	burlesque	滑稽讽刺作品
42	libretto	(歌剧或音乐剧的)唱词,歌词
43	testimony	证据;证明
44	between the lines	言外之意
45	stupendous	惊人的;巨大的
46	hold the stage	引人注目;继续上演
47	compromise	妥协;折中
48	conceive	设想;怀孕
49	downright	彻底地;完全地
50	torment	(肉体、精神上的)折磨,痛苦
51	bail out	保释;帮助……摆脱困境

	English	Chinese
52	prior to	在……之前
53	undercut	以低于……的价格销售
54	palpable	明显的
55	penetration	渗透
56	blanket	通用的
57	gigantic	巨大的
58	devaluation	贬值
59	quota	限额
60	spark	引发
61	prominent	重要的
62	ward off	防止
63	deter	阻止
64	wrangle over	争论
65	acute problem	尖锐的问题
66	erode	侵蚀
67	inherit a legacy	继承遗产
68	contentious	有争议的
69	straws in the wind	征兆;苗头
70	retaliation	报复
71	dry up	干涸
72	ambivalent	矛盾的
73	reverse	逆转
74	layoff	裁员
75	lubricant	润滑剂
76	follow suit	跟着做;模仿
77	tariff	关税
78	orders of magnitude	数量级

	English	Chinese
79	stem from	根源在于；起源于
80	deterioration	恶化
81	recession	经济衰退
82	intrusion	侵入
83	boycott	抵制
84	throwback	返祖者；返祖现象
85	attendant	伴随的；随之产生的
86	permissible	允许的
87	in jeopardy	处于危险之中
88	dismantle	分解
89	mandate	命令
90	be riddled with	充满；充斥
91	add fuel to the fire	火上浇油
92	implosion	内爆；向心聚爆
93	monkey wrench	活动扳手；破坏性因素
94	a body blow	巨大打击
95	meltdown	崩溃；垮台
96	lead the charge	控制；率领
97	looming	迫近的
98	outbreak	爆发
99	container ship	集装箱船
100	momentum	势头

Word List 30

	English	Chinese
1	stance	（尤指公开表明的）观点，立场

	English	Chinese
2	assemble	聚集;收集
3	furtive	偷偷摸摸的;鬼鬼祟祟的
4	tan	晒成棕褐色的肤色
5	close-cropped	(头发或草)剪得很短的
6	vile	糟透的;邪恶的
7	repose	休息;镇静
8	snowbound	被大雪困住的;被大雪封住的
9	bonsai	盆景
10	prune	修剪(树枝)
11	facsimile	摹本;复制本
12	acknowledge	承认;告知收悉
13	cache	贮藏物;隐藏物
14	kickshaw	无价值的饰物;华而不实的东西
15	awkwardly	局促不安地;尴尬地
16	stump	树墩;残余部分
17	scab	(伤口上结的)痂
18	forceps	(医用的)镊子,钳子
19	shard	(玻璃、金属等的)碎片
20	disinfectant	消毒剂;杀菌剂
21	inert	无活动能力的;无行动力的
22	athwart	横跨于
23	scramble	争夺;抢夺
24	dome	穹顶;穹顶建筑
25	probe	探究;详尽调查
26	heft	举起;抬起
27	accomplice	共犯;帮凶
28	oatmeal	燕麦粥;燕麦片

	English	Chinese
29	deceased	已死的;亡故的
30	dignified	庄重的;有尊严的
31	solid	扎实的;可信赖的
32	unwrap	拆开……的包装
33	make one's rounds	巡视
34	prop up	扶持;支持（某人）
35	peculiarity	怪癖;特点
36	dwell	居住,栖身
37	deliver	运送;投递
38	disinfect	给……消毒
39	gaze	（文学批评用语）视角
40	irony	反语;反话
41	burn your fingers	没有先见之明而蒙受损失
42	spy on	暗中监视;窥探
43	dwarf	矮子;侏儒
44	speculate	猜测;投机
45	ponder	沉思;考虑
46	reckon	想;认为
47	exhaustive	彻底的;详尽的
48	proceed	继续进行;继续做
49	trial	审判;审理
50	verdict	（陪审团的）裁定,裁决
51	gambit	开头一着;开局策略
52	huddle	挤作一团;聚在一起
53	preemptive	先发制人的
54	proliferation	大量
55	coercive	强制的

	English	Chinese
56	stricture	限制
57	endorsement	赞同；支持
58	yak about	喋喋不休
59	get a boost	提升
60	shrug off	摆脱；不理睬
61	hard-liner	强硬路线者
62	animated	活跃的
63	stash	藏匿；隐藏
64	bode	预兆
65	blink	眨眼
66	centrifuge	离心机
67	undermine	（海、风等）侵蚀……的基础
68	dismiss	不理会
69	jangle	（使）烦躁不安
70	hawkish	鹰派的；主战的
71	intransigence	不妥协；不让步
72	belligerence	好战；好斗
73	mete out	给予惩罚；责罚
74	moderate	温和的
75	ratchet	逐步增加；逐步增强
76	unveil	揭示
77	concede	（通常指不情愿地）承认
78	weather	平安度过（难关）
79	unsettled	不稳定的
80	bar	禁止
81	execute	执行
82	unilateral	单边的

	English	**Chinese**
83	defiance	违抗
84	trot out	翻出（老套的借口、解释等）
85	face-off	对峙；对抗
86	nudge	轻推
87	hamper	妨碍
88	alienate	使疏远
89	muddle through	应付过去
90	soothe	缓和
91	astonish	使大为惊奇
92	roadblock	路障
93	pundit	博学的人
94	jeopardize	危害
95	high-profile	经常出镜（或见报）的
96	be poised to	准备就绪
97	the devil is in the details	细节决定成败
98	show little stomach for	对……不感兴趣
99	at loggerheads with	发生争执
100	no mean	出色的；了不起的

Word List 31

	English	**Chinese**
1	myth	神话；神话故事
2	inaugural	就职的；就任的
3	reaffirm	重申；再次确定
4	creed	信条；信念；教义

	English	Chinese
5	bleak	(地方)荒凉的；(境况)惨淡的
6	aspiration	抱负；渴望
7	consensus	一致的意见；共识
8	indefensible	无可辩解的；站不住脚的
9	hoax	恶作剧；骗局
10	lull	使放松；使镇静
11	complacency	自满；自鸣得意
12	oddity	怪事；反常现象
13	egalitarian	平等主义者
14	disparity	不均等；不一致
15	minuscule	微小的；极小的
16	democratize	使民主化
17	spectrum	光谱；频谱
18	segregation	(种族、宗教等的)隔离
19	stagnate	停滞不前；不发展
20	affluent	富裕的；富足的
21	reverse	颠倒；彻底转变
22	gut	肠道；消化道
23	discharge	允许出院；释放
24	condemn	(通常指出于道义而)谴责，指责
25	brink	边缘；始发点
26	deception	骗术；骗局
27	magnitude	巨大；重要性
28	diminish	减少；降低
29	unconscionable	违背良心的
30	contingent on	决定于；取决于
31	robust	坚定的

	English	Chinese
32	suffice	足够；满足要求
33	contemporary	当代的；现代的
34	imperative	极重要的；迫切的
35	true to	忠实于
36	alternative	可供选择的；可替代的
37	commitment	保证；承诺
38	surpass	超过；胜过
39	accurate	正确无误的
40	reconcile sth. with sth.	使和谐一致
41	restrain	阻止；遏制
42	restrict	限制；限定；妨碍
43	confine	监禁；禁闭
44	deviate	背离；偏离
45	divert	使转向；使绕道
46	immerse	使浸没于
47	submerge	使浸入（水中）；淹没
48	eligible	有资格的；合格的
49	illegible	难辨认的；字迹模糊的
50	eminent	成功的；著名的
51	posture	立场
52	halt	停止
53	trajectory	飞行轨道；轨迹
54	engender	造成；导致
55	underestimation	低估
56	sobering	使人清醒的
57	folly	耗费巨大而无得益的事
58	inconceivable	难以置信的

	English	Chinese
59	agenda	议程
60	resurgent	复兴的
61	tug of war	拔河
62	maritime	海运的
63	attendant	服务员;侍者
64	rival	竞争对手
65	counterbalance	抗衡;抵消
66	dissolve	溶解
67	misapprehension	误解;误会
68	contain	抑制（感情）
69	cloak	掩饰;幌子
70	nominal	名义上的
71	displace	取代
72	hazard	危险
73	initiate	（通过特别仪式）正式接纳
74	a cascade of	一连串的
75	large-scale	大范围的
76	miscalculation	误算
77	steeple	（教堂的）尖塔
78	dynamic	有干劲的;精力充沛的
79	entitlement	权利;资格
80	sway	控制力;影响
81	agency	代理行;经销处
82	Thucydides's Trap	修昔底德陷阱
83	inexorable	不可变更的
84	pertinent	相关的
85	clout	影响力;势力

	English	Chinese
86	synergy	协同增效
87	pivot	枢轴；支点
88	state visit	国事访问
89	entanglement	瓜葛；牵连
90	leave sb. little choice but to	使某人别无选择
91	prowess	高超的技艺
92	be shorn of	被剥夺
93	ascendancy	支配地位；优势
94	a succession of	一连串的
95	geostrategic	地缘战略学的
96	millennium	一千年
97	magnitude	巨大；重大
98	business as usual	一切正常；一切照常
99	chronicle	编年史；年代记
100	stakeholder	股东；利益相关者

Word List 32

	English	Chinese
1	nude	裸体的
2	awakening	醒悟；觉醒
3	peer through	透过……看
4	in search of	寻找
5	explosive	炸药
6	graphic	形象的
7	anatomically	在结构上；在解剖上

	English	Chinese
8	blur	(使)模糊
9	blurt	脱口而出
10	indignant	愤慨的
11	in the wake of	随着……而来
12	poll	民意测验
13	approve of	赞成
14	effusive	太动感情的
15	pledge	誓言
16	commissioner	(委员会的)委员
17	in light of	考虑到;鉴于
18	invasive	侵袭的;扩散的
19	mince	剁碎;绞碎
20	strip search	光身搜查(看是否携藏毒品、武器等)
21	outrage	暴行
22	illusion	错觉
23	contraband	走私品;走私货
24	mannequin	(商店中用于陈列服装的)人体模型
25	blob	一滴;一小团
26	skeptic	怀疑宗教(尤指基督教)者
27	blot	吸干(墨水等);揿干
28	prosthetic	修复术的;假体的
29	precondition	先决条件;前提
30	cavity	洞;腔
31	vendor	(某种产品的)销售公司
32	oversight	负责;照管
33	intrusive	侵入的
34	creep	讨厌鬼

	English	Chinese
35	tabloid	通俗小报
36	rogue	骗子；恶棍
37	troll	搜寻；搜查
38	hypothetical	假设的
39	embattled	被困扰的；危机四伏的
40	nominee	被提名人
41	estranged	（夫妻）分居的
42	nomination	提名
43	ephemeral	短暂的
44	project	投射；投影
45	on the instructions of	按指示
46	overwhelmingly	压倒性的；无法抗拒的
47	confidential	机密的
48	give sb. the illusion	给某人错觉
49	failed attempt	失败的尝试
50	randomly	随机地
51	sectoral	部门的；行业的
52	dignity	尊严
53	slum	贫民窟
54	shanty	棚屋
55	mobilize	动员
56	prosperity	繁荣
57	perpetuate	使持续
58	precisely	精确地
59	desperately	极端地
60	tackle	解决
61	flaunt	炫耀

	English	Chinese
62	carry on	继续
63	irredeemably	不可救药地
64	spoil	破坏
65	aspire	渴望
66	untapped	未开发的
67	halve	使减半
68	reservoir	水库
69	continuum	连续体
70	pleading	恳求
71	footprint	足迹
72	inhabit	栖息;居住于
73	transparent	透明的
74	entrepreneurship	企业家精神
75	hold sth./sb. in check	控制;制止
76	scenario	设想;方案
77	fulfill	实现
78	put a premium on	重视;珍视
79	prerequisite	先决条件
80	unsustainable	不可持续的
81	concession	让步;妥协
82	sacrifice	牺牲
83	toxic	有毒的
84	coalition	联盟;同盟
85	labour-intensive	劳动密集型的
86	flicker	闪烁;闪现
87	life-or-death	生死攸关的
88	depletion	用光;耗尽

	English	Chinese
89	oppression	压迫
90	initiative	主动权优势；有利地位
91	misrule	管理不善
92	respiratory	呼吸的
93	conventional	常规的
94	obstinate	棘手的
95	handout	捐赠品；救济品
96	privileged	享有特权的
97	at the expense of	以……为代价
98	vicious circle	恶性循环
99	be infected	被感染
100	on fair terms	公平地

Part Three
Selected Readings

Reading Assignment

A Tale of Two Cities

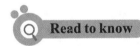

1. What is the setting of *A Tale of Two Cities* and what historical events does it cover?
2. Who are the main characters in *A Tale of Two Cities* and what are their roles in the story?

3. How does Dickens use the motif of duality in *A Tale of Two Cities*?
4. Discuss the theme of sacrifice in *A Tale of Two Cities* and how it drives the plot.

5. Imagine an alternative ending for *A Tale of Two Cities*. How would you rewrite the conclusion of the story?

Reading Assignment 2

Jane Eyre

Read to know

1. What is the setting of *Jane Eyre* and how does it contribute to the atmosphere of the story?

2. What are some key events or plots that shape Jane Eyre's journey and development throughout the novel?

Read to reason

3. What are some major themes explored in *Jane Eyre*?

4. How does the character of Jane Eyre challenge societal norms and expectations?

Read to create

5. Write an alternate ending for *Jane Eyre* where Jane chooses a different path for her future.

Reading Assignment 3

Pride and Prejudice

Read to know

1. What is the social and historical context of *Pride and Prejudice*?
2. How did Jane Austen's unique narrative style contribute to the enduring popularity of *Pride and Prejudice*?

Read to reason

3. What are the main themes explored in *Pride and Prejudice*?
4. How does the character of Elizabeth Bennet challenge societal expectations and norms?

Read to create

5. Write a letter from one of the minor characters in *Pride and Prejudice* to a friend, sharing their perspective on the events of the novel and their thoughts on the main characters.

Reading Assignment 4

Robinson Crusoe

Read to know

1. What are some of the major influences of Daniel Defoe's writing *Robinson Crusoe*?
2. In what ways does *Robinson Crusoe* reflect the colonial mindset of the time?

Read to reason

3. What are the themes explored in *Robinson Crusoe*?

4. If you were stranded on a deserted island like Robinson Crusoe, what three items would you want to have with you and why?

Read to create

5. Write a short dialogue between Robinson Crusoe and his loyal companion, Friday, discussing their plans for survival on the island.

Reading Assignment 5

A Passage to India

Read to know

1. Who are the main characters in *A Passage to India* and what are their backgrounds and motivations?

2. What is the setting of the novel?

Read to reason

3. How does E. M. Forster explore the themes of cultural misunderstanding and miscommunication in *A Passage to India*?

4. What role do the Marabar Caves play in the narrative and the characters' experiences? How do they symbolize the mysteries and complexities of India?

Read to create

5. If you were to rewrite the ending of *A Passage to India*, how would you change it and why?

○○○○○ Part Three Selected Readings

Reading Assignment

The Old Man and the Sea

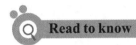

1. What is the central conflict in *The Old Man and the Sea*?
2. What is Ernest Hemingway's writing style?

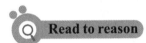

3. How does Santiago's relationship with the boy, Manolin, contribute to the story's themes?
4. What symbolic devices are used to enhance the depth and meaning of the novel?

5. Write a prequel to *The Old Man and the Sea* that explores Santiago's earlier life and experiences as a fisherman.

Reading Assignment

Lord of the Flies

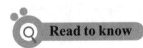

1. What is the significance of the title *Lord of the Flies* in the novel?
2. What is the main conflict in the novel *Lord of the Flies*?

Read to reason

3. What are some of the major themes explored in *Lord of the Flies*?

4. How does the author use symbolism in *Lord of the Flies* to convey deeper meanings?

Read to create

5. Imagine an alternate ending for *Lord of the Flies*. How would the story unfold differently?

Reading Assignment 8

Gulliver's Travels

Read to know

1. What is the main plot of *Gulliver's Travels* and what are the different lands that Gulliver visits?

2. What are some of the major themes explored in *Gulliver's Travels*?

Read to reason

3. How does Swift use satire in *Gulliver's Travels* to criticize society and human nature?

4. In what ways does Gulliver's interaction with the Houyhnhnms challenge readers to examine the limitations of human society?

Read to create

5. Imagine a new land for Gulliver to visit in a sequel to *Gulliver's Travels*. What would this new land be like and what societal flaws could it satirize?

Part Three　Selected Readings

Reading Assignment 9

The Scarlet Letter

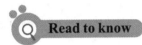

1. What are the stylistic features of *The Scarlet Letter*?
2. What are symbolic meanings of "needlework" and the scarlet letter "A"?

3. How to interpret Hester Prynne's return from Europe to America?
4. Does Hester get rebirth in *The Scarlet Letter*?

5. How to understand sin and redemption in *The Scarlet Letter*?

Reading Assignment 10

Tess of the d' Urbervilles

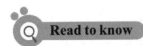

1. What are the stylistic features of *Tess of the d' Urbervilles*?
2. Collect the words and phrases the author employed to modify Tess, and analyze the character of Tess.

179

Read to reason

3. The vivid discription of environment is one of the stylistic features, please pick up one or two examples to analyze.

4. What are symbolic meanings of "bird" in *Tess of the d' Urbervilles*? Please give some examples to illustrate it.

Read to create

5. What are the causes of Tess's tragedy?

Reading Assignment 11

The Adventure of Huckleberry Finn

Read to know

1. What are the stylistic features of *The Adventure of Huckleberry Finn*?
2. What are the symbolic meanings of the Mississippi River?

Read to reason

3. What are the themes of *The Adventure of Huckleberry Finn*?
4. What are the images of Huck and Jim?

Read to create

5. One of the stylistic features of this fiction is the use of black English. Please discuss the features and functions of black English.

Part Three Selected Readings

Reading Assignment 12

Vanity Fair

Read to know

1. In *Vanity Fair*, how the most impressive female characters, namely, Rebecca Sharp and Amelia Sedley are made?

2. What are the writing characteristics of *Vanity Fair*?

Read to reason

3. What are narrative strategies of *Vanity Fair*?

4. Metaphor is widely used in *Vanity Fair*. How metaphors are used to make the characters vivid?

Read to create

5. How irony is employed in *Vanity Fair* by Thackeray to make the novel attractive?

Reading Assignment 13

Frankenstein

Read to know

1. What is the theme of *Frankenstein*?

2. What are symbolic meanings of "fire" in *Frankenstein*? Please give some examples to illustrate it.

Read to reason

3. Why *Frankenstein* is regarded as a tragedy?
4. What is the realistic meaning of *Frankenstein* ?

Read to create

5. What are features of narration in *Frankenstein* ?

Reading Assignment 14

The Great Gatsby

Read to know

1. What is the Gatsby's "American Dream"?
2. Discuss the usages of symbolism in *The Great Gatsby*. Please give some examples to illustrate it.

Read to reason

3. What caused the destruction of "American Dream"?
4. What are the symbolic meanings of "car" in *The Great Gatsby*?

Read to create

5. What is the tragedy of Gatsby and how does the author present it?

Part Three Selected Readings

Reading Assignment 15

Dubliners

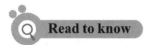

1. What is the theme of *Dubliners*?
2. What rhetoric devices are employed in *Dubliners*? Please list some examples to illustrate it.

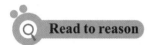

3. How a style of a scrupulous meanness is presented by repetition?
4. What are the writing techniques employed in *Dubliners*?

5. What is the symbolic meaning of light in *Dubliners* by Joyce?

Reading Assignment 16

Heart of Darkness

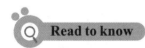

1. What are the narrative techniques in *Heart of Darkness*?
2. What does "light" represent and what is "darkness" in *Heart of Darkness*?

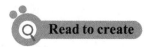

Read to reason

3. How the frame narrative pattern is revealed in *Heart of Darkness*?
4. What is the symbolic meaning of "heart" in *Heart of Darkness*?

Read to create

5. What is the nature of the main character Marlow in *Heart of Darkness*?

Part Four
Passage Dictation

Passage Dictation

Reading is not only enjoyable; it is also beneficial to your health. Reading is similar to mental exercise. Reading makes your mind strong and healthy, just as it makes your muscles strong and healthy. Reading enables you to use your imagination, which is a stress-free activity. Reading also enhances your intelligence. You can acquire new knowledge. You can also master new vocabulary. Reading helps you memorize. It aids in training the brain to concentrate. People who read often are more adept at problem solving and at writing. Reading also makes you feel more at ease. What is your favorite aspect of reading?

Passage Dictation

I'm actually looking at a picture of Alice. In the picture, she's not at home. She's in a park. She is sitting on a bench. She is eating her lunch. Some young men and women are running on the grass in the park. In front of Alice, a squirrel is sitting on the ground. The squirrel is eating nuts. When Alice eats lunch in the park, she is always watching the squirrel. In the picture, ducks are swimming in the pond and birds are flying in the sky. A police officer is riding a horse. He rides his horse in the park every day. A family is having a picnic near Alice. They go on picnics every week.

Passage Dictation 3

Happiness is perhaps the most important goal of human life. The concept of happiness has been the center of debate among philosophers. To promote the right of citizens to pursue happiness, legislators have enacted laws. Advertisers on television, radio, and in the press tell consumers that a variety of things will make them happy. Interestingly, people tend to think they are happier than those around them and believe they will be happy in the future. Most people expect that in ten years they will be happier than they are now.

It's clear that everyone, from writers and philosophers to lawmakers and ordinary people, gives a lot of thought to happiness.

Passage Dictation 4

Each year, more and more "baby boomers" reach age 65 and become eligible for Medicare. As of July 2009, about 13 percent of the U. S. population was age 65 or older, according to the Census Bureau. The percentage of the population in this group is expected to increase to 21 percent by 2050. Medicare is especially important for seniors as health care costs increase and needs grow with age.

Medicare helps seniors access some of the best health care in the world. However, it also comes with a huge financial toll, so younger generations should consider preventative care to improve their golden years.

Passage Dictation 5

The ladybug is a type of insect. Like all insects, it has six legs. The ladybug has two pairs of wings. The outer wings are hard and are used for protection. Ladybugs use their inner wings to fly. Although most people associate ladybugs with red and black spots, this is not true of all species. They can also be orange and black or yellow and black. Some ladybugs have no spots at all, but their spots may resemble stripes. Ladybugs' spots and bright colors aren't just for show. Their purpose is to warn potential attackers that this beetle has a terrible taste. Ladybugs are beneficial insects in the garden. They eat other bugs that may harm vegetable plants.

Passage Dictation

Every day, millions of shoppers rush into stores, both online and in person, in search of the perfect gift. Last year, Americans spent more than $30 billion at retail stores in December alone. In addition to holiday gifts, most people purchase gifts for other occasions throughout the year, such as weddings, birthdays, anniversaries, graduations, and baby showers. Frequent gift-giving experiences can create conflicting emotions for the giver. Many look forward to the opportunity to purchase a gift because it is a powerful way to strengthen bonds with those closest to them. At the same time, many anxiously consider that the gift they purchase will disappoint rather than delight the recipient.

Passage Dictation

People trade because they need or desire items they do not have. People also trade for work they cannot accomplish on their own. Countries trade with each other for the same reason. For example, some countries have natural resources such as coal, oil, or wood that other countries may wish to purchase. These countries try to sell excess goods, products, or services to other countries. They make money from these sales and use the money to buy items they need but cannot produce themselves. International trade benefits both producers and consumers. On the one hand, they can make more money, and on the other hand, consumers in other countries can purchase cheaper goods.

Passage Dictation 8

Happiness is not an innate trait; rather, it can be learned and become a habit. According to scientists, adopting new routines and behaviors can significantly improve a person's level of happiness. People can learn how to become happier by engaging in a variety of activities, such as socializing, watching fun movies or reading interesting books, keeping a gratitude journal, participating in enjoyable activities such as sports, hobbies, or the arts, focusing on positive outcomes, and doing kind things for others. This is true even though people rarely change their basic temperament. Making others happy seems to make you happy.

Passage Dictation 9

All creatures are capable of communicating with their own species through different sounds, body language, or smells. Communication usually involves behaviors related to daily life or survival, such as identifying or defending territory, searching for mates, and sounding danger warnings. Although the warning sounds of birds and groundhogs contain a great deal of information about the nature of the threat, only some of these language skills are shared by animals and humans. Why is this so? A small part of the reason is the structure of the throat, but the main reason is the structure of the brain.

Passage Dictation 10

Kim had hiked the mountains many times. She loved the challenge of the trail—the gnarled roots that might trip her up, the rocks worn smooth by years of footsteps. Her brother Ned leapt ahead of her like a mountain goat on the trail. He had probably reached Alpine Lake, the sparkling, immaculate blue lake that was their destination. When she stepped off the wooded trail and caught her first glimpse of the lake, she stopped to admire its beauty.

Passage Dictation 11

The dropout rate in some American high schools is as high as 50 percent. There are many reasons why students drop out. Two-thirds of dropouts suffer from a lack of motivation to learn. They simply cannot study hard enough. Nearly half of the students miss so many classes that they are unable to keep up. Many students were not adequately prepared at their previous schools. One-third of students believe that getting a job is more important than finishing school. High school dropouts face more challenges in society and in their future lives. They are more likely to be unemployed or in poverty. There is also a large income gap between high school dropouts and graduates.

Passage Dictation 12

Maybe you live in a flat in the city, or maybe you live in a trailer in the country. There are all kinds of homes all over the world. Some are big. Some are very small. Some houses are built with wood and stone. Some houses are built with brick or mud. Some houses near the sea are built on stilts to avoid flooding. In some areas of extreme heat, houses were built underground. Many people live in houses that were not designed with relocation in mind. In some parts of the world, people must move from one place to another in search of food or work.

Passage Dictation 13

The Moon is composed of rocks. If you walk on the surface of the Moon, you will notice that the first layer is a thick layer of dust. Your boots will sink a little in the dust and leave boot prints. These prints will not fade because there is no wind on the Moon. Under the first layer of dust is hard rock. The core of the Moon is made of iron and is located in the center of the Moon. There are many round holes in the surface of the Moon. There are also mountains and "seas" on the Moon. These "seas" are different from our oceans, which are made of water. On the other hand, the Moon's seas are made of hard lava.

Passage Dictation

Beijing, formerly known as Peking, is the capital of the People's Republic of China and one of the most populous cities in the world. Beijing is the political, cultural, and educational center of China and the headquarters of most large state-owned enterprises in China. With the world's largest central square, Tian'anmen Square, the largest and best-preserved imperial palace complex, the Forbidden City, the well-preserved Great Wall of China, and the world's largest sacrificial complex, the Temple of Heaven, Beijing attracts both domestic and foreign tourists, who come to marvel at its centuries-old history and unique cultural heritage.

Passage Dictation

Adults need at least six hours of sleep each night, experts say. If you don't get enough sleep, you'll feel sleepy throughout the day. Young children need at least 9 hours of sleep a night. After-school activities can take away from children's sleep. In addition, parents with busy lives often stay up late, and so do their children. Sleep-deprived children have a hard time falling asleep at night, which affects their daily routines and makes them less active and productive during the school day.

Passage Dictation

In some countries, governments control all trade, while in others, companies and businesses are free to trade. However, all governments have some degree of control over trade. Governments may prohibit companies from buying or selling dangerous or illegal products or military technology. When companies grow in size, they often acquire other companies and create monopolies. Governments enact laws to prevent companies from becoming too powerful and controlling markets. Many governments try to help their industries by making it harder to import foreign goods. Governments may also limit the number of products they buy from other countries to protect their own companies and industries.

Part Five
Mini-Lectures

Mini-Lecture 1

The Little Risks You Can Take to Increase Your Luck

I. What is luck?

1) Luck is defined as success or failure (1) _____ by chance.

2) We rarely see all the (2) _____ that come into play to make people lucky.

II. How do you catch the winds of luck?

1) Be willing to take small risks that get you out of your (3) _____.

2) Understand that everyone who helps you on your journey is playing (4) _____ in getting you to your goals.

3) I feel incredibly (5) _____, and I promise you it has increased my luck.

III. Changing your relationship with ideas

1) The (6) _____ are often something truly remarkable.

2) The ventures that are really (7) _____ around you... They all started out as crazy ideas.

(1) _____
(2) _____
(3) _____
(4) _____
(5) _____
(6) _____
(7) _____

3) Sometimes people were born into (8) _____. 4) Luck is a (9) _____ that hits us with something wonderful or something terrible. Ⅳ. Conclusion If you're willing to really go out and (10) _____ and willing to really look at ideas...you can build a bigger and bigger sail to catch the winds of luck.	(8) _____ (9) _____ (10) _____

Mini-Lecture 2

The Riddle of Experience VS. Memory Ⅰ. Introduction There are several cognitive traps that sort of make it almost impossible to (1) _____ about happiness. Ⅱ. Cognitive traps 1) The first of these traps is a reluctance to (2) _____. 2) The second trap is a confusion between (3) _____. 3) The third is the (4) _____. Example: What it (5) _____ were the memories of the experience... He had had 20 minutes of (6) _____. Ⅲ. In terms of two selves 1) An experiencing self is capable of (7) _____. 2) The remembering self starts with a (8) _____ of our memories. Ⅳ. A direct conflict 1) The biggest difference between them is in the (9) _____. 2) Time is actually the (10) _____ that distinguishes a remembering self from an experiencing self.	(1) _____ (2) _____ (3) _____ (4) _____ (5) _____ (6) _____ (7) _____ (8) _____ (9) _____ (10) _____

Part Five Mini-Lectures

Mini-Lecture 3

Why do We Dream?

I. The purpose of our dreams

Are they strictly random brain impulses, or as a sort of (1) _____?

II. Why do we dream?

1) Early civilizations thought dream worlds were real, (2) _____ that they could enter.

2) Those theories essentially fall into two categories:

a. The first is the idea that dreams are only (3) _____.

b. Psychological theories are based on the idea that dreaming allows us to (4) _____.

3) Perhaps it is a (5) _____ of the two theories.

III. Dreaming and the brain

1) We go through (6) _____.

2) Our brain activity throughout these stages is (7) _____.

IV. How to improve your dream recall

1) Tell yourself you will (8) _____.

2) Keep a (9) _____ next to your bed.

3) Wake up slowly to (10) _____ the "mood" of your last dream.

(1) _____
(2) _____
(3) _____
(4) _____
(5) _____
(6) _____
(7) _____
(8) _____
(9) _____
(10) _____

Mini-Lecture 4

The Changes Facing Fast Food

I. Fast-food firms have to be a thick-skinned bunch.

1) Health experts (1) _____ them.

2) These are things fast-food firms have learned to (2) _____.

(1) _____
(2) _____

Ⅱ. Recession-proof 1) Cheap meals become even more attractive. 2) Traffic was boosted in America, the home of fast food, with (3) _____. Ⅲ. Results 1) Fast-food chains have (4) _____ better than their more expensive competitors. 2) Not all fast-food companies have been (5) _____. 3) Some fast-food companies also (6) _____ their own profits. 4) Fast-food firms have cleverly avoided (7) _____. Ⅳ. Strategies 1) Many are now introducing (8) _____. 2) Get customers to buy (9) _____ items. 3) Many see breakfast as a (10) _____.	(3) _____ (4) _____ (5) _____ (6) _____ (7) _____ (8) _____ (9) _____ (10) _____

Mini-Lecture 5

Is Breakfast Really the Most Important Meal of the Day? Ⅰ. Introduction 1) It is widely considered wrong not to eat breakfast. 2) Believing that (1) _____ is a serious mistake. Ⅱ. Different opinions 1) Eating a balanced breakfast helps to (2) _____. 2) There have been concerns around the (3) _____. Ⅲ. What's the reality? 1) Is breakfast a necessary start to the day or a (4) _____? 2) Who made breakfast the (5) _____ of the day were more likely to have a lower body mass index. 3) It was unclear if breakfast-skippers were just more likely to be overweight.	(1) _____ (2) _____ (3) _____ (4) _____ (5) _____

Part Five Mini-Lectures

  4) It was changing their (6)_____. (6)_____

Ⅳ. Conclusion

  1) Breakfast-skippers have been found to be (7)_____ (7)_____
about nutrition and health.

  2) The time we eat influences body weight. (8)_____

  3) Breakfast is also associated with (8)_____.

  4) High-protein breakfasts have been found (9)_____. (9)_____

  5) But getting (10)_____ throughout the day is more
important. (10)_____

Mini-Lecture

Is It Really OK to Eat Food Dropped on the Floor?

Ⅰ. Introduction. (1)_____

  1) Is five seconds on the floor (1)_____?

  2) Women were more likely than men to eat food that (2)_____
(2)_____ on the floor.

Ⅱ. What does science tell us? (3)_____

  1) They reported bacteria (3)_____ from the tiles to the
cookies within five seconds. (4)_____

  2) The overall number of bacteria on the surface (4)_____.

  3) The kind of surface (5)_____ as well. (5)_____

  Example: Carpets seem to be (6)_____ places to drop your
food than wood or tile. (6)_____

Ⅲ. Should you eat food fallen on the floor then?

  1) 0.1% is still enough to make you sick. (7)_____

  2) Certain types of bacteria are (7)_____.

  Example: 10 bacteria or less of an especially deadly strain of (8)_____
bacteria can cause severe illness and death in people with
(8)_____ systems. (9)_____

  3) Bacteria are carried by (9)_____, moist surfaces.

195

IV. Conclusion Research or (10) _____ tells us that the the best thing to do is keep your hands, utensils and other surfaces clean.	(10) _____

Mini-Lecture 7

Team Spirit I. Teamwork is becoming popular 1) Teams have become the (1) _____ of organizations. 2) Companies are abandoning (2) _____ departments. 3) A network of teams is replacing the conventional hierarchy. II. The reasons for the fashion for teams 1) The old way of organising people is (3) _____. 2) Technological innovation places greater value on agility. 3) Digital technology also makes it easier to co-ordinate activities without (4) _____ hierarchy Example: The fashion for teams is also (5) _____ from hospital to the US Army. III. Problems 1) Teamwork may also lead to (6) _____ and poor decision-making. 2) Teams are (7) _____ by problems of co-ordination and motivation. Example: High-flyers forced to work in teams may be (8) _____ and free-riders empowered. Groupthink may be unavoidable. IV. Solution 1) Having a strong (9) _____. 2) To give employees (10) _____. 3) Some work is best left to the individual.	(1) _____ (2) _____ (3) _____ (4) _____ (5) _____ (6) _____ (7) _____ (8) _____ (9) _____ (10) _____

Mini-Lecture 8

How to Learn Any Language with an App I. Apps are all the rage nowadays 　· Keeping fit 　· Organizing your schedule 　· Communicating with friends 　· Even learning a language II. Educational apps are becoming increasingly popular 　1) As (1)_____ to traditional education. 　2) It's (2)_____ to learn on a pocket-sized device. 　3) Apps are a (3)_____ through which a language can be studied. 　4) The way you use them will (4)_____ how successful you are. 　Example: Flicking nonchalantly makes slow progress; the avid reader will (5)_____. III. Suggestions 　1) Use apps extensively, but not (6)_____. 　2) Establish your purpose and (7)_____. 　3) Don't forget your purpose and own, (8)_____. 　4) Feedback is truly, madly, (9)_____. 　5) Make it social. IV. Conclusion 　The combination of app, language school, friends, evenings out, and a choice book or two proved (10)_____.	(1)_____ (2)_____ (3)_____ (4)_____ (5)_____ (6)_____ (7)_____ (8)_____ (9)_____ (10)_____

Mini-Lecture 9

Stress Stress is a condition (1)_____ mental or emotional tension.	(1)_____

1) Almost 2/3 American workers are struggling or suffering stress from the (2)_____.	(2)_____
2) Almost 1/2 American workers expressed concern about their ability to provide for (3)_____.	(3)_____
Ⅰ. Stress effect	
1) Some unavoidable stress can keep our (4)_____ strong.	(4)_____
2) Too much stress may make an existing health problem worse or can (5)_____ if a person is at risk for the condition.	(5)_____
Ⅱ. Causes of stress	
1) It can be (6)_____, such as injury or disease.	(6)_____
2) It can be mental, such as problems involving your family, job, health or (7)_____.	(7)_____
Ⅲ. Several ways to deal with stress	
· Deep breathing and a method of guided thought called (8)_____	(8)_____
· Exercise, eating healthy foods, getting enough rest and (9)_____ spent working and playing	(9)_____
Ⅳ. Conclusion	
People should attempt to accept or change stressful situations (10)_____.	(10)_____

Mini-Lecture 10

How the West Views Our Animals	
How does a westerner see each of the 12 animals in the Chinese zodiac?	
Rat: Most people see (1)_____ in the creature.	(1)_____
Ox:	
1) Oxen are respected for its strength and hard-working spirit.	(2)_____
2) Bulls are generally viewed (2)_____ because of their aggressive nature.	

198

3) Cows are considered the "cutest" one. Tiger: Tigers are also used to describe (3)_____. Rabbit: Rabbits are known as being (4)_____. Horse: In the US, they may be kept as (5)_____ by people. Sheep: Sheep are viewed (6)_____ and also carry the image of a "follower". Monkey: In the US, a monkey has been used as (7)_____ that refers to African-Americans. Rooster: 1) A rooster is strong and proud. 2) (8)_____ is viewed as weak, or even stupid. Dog: "Man's best friends", but sometimes a dog is used cruelly to refer to (9)_____. Boar: 1) "Boar" usually refers to a wild pig. 2) "Pig" most often refers to the farm-raised animal, (10)_____.	(3)_____ (4)_____ (5)_____ (6)_____ (7)_____ (8)_____ (9)_____ (10)_____

Mini-Lecture 11

How to Control Jealousy? Ⅰ. What is jealousy? Jealousy is an (1)_____ and almost seems involuntary. Ⅱ. Some tips that can help in controlling jealousy · Count your blessings A good way is to start making a list of different things we (2)_____ that a lot of other people have not, even general things that we really (3)_____. · Trade-offs Everything comes as part of (4)_____.	(1)_____ (2)_____ (3)_____ (4)_____

1) If somebody has something that you don't, you also have a few things that they don't. 2) (5)_____ other things can achieved a lot of things. · Take inspiration 　Make a list of those people who would be (6) _____ when you achieve something. · They have worked hard for it 　It is always good to (7) _____ others' hard work and appreciate it so they do the same for you when time comes. · Give 　1) Give a person something nice, if you constantly (8) _____ them. 　2) After that, whenever you see them being happy, you'll realize that you (9) _____ their overall happiness. Ⅲ. Conclusion 　Most importantly, challenge jealousy in (10) _____ emotions.	(5)_____ (6)_____ (7)_____ (8)_____ (9)_____ (10)_____

Mini-Lecture

Why Is a Job a Hard Thing to Find? 　Employment for university graduates has remained (1) _____ for the Chinese government. 　The 2009 Employment Blue Book of University Graduates shows that even when the job market was performing well, (2) _____ for fresh graduates remained low. Ⅰ. Demand-supply difference 　1) Many blame (3)_____ for rising graduate unemployment. 　2) Some blame the (4) _____ for the cold spell on the domestic white-collar human resources market. Ⅱ. Changes in thinking required 　1) Industrially speaking, (5)_____ is the largest employer of fresh graduates.	(1)_____ (2)_____ (3)_____ (4)_____ (5)_____

2) Another limitation is that few wish to work in (6)_____ of the country.

Ⅲ. Talent shortage

Take engineers for example:

1) Chinese job applicants have (7)_____ than practical skills.

2) Chinese students rarely participate in (8)_____ to solve practical problems like European and North American students.

3) Chinese students also need to improve their (9)_____.

Ⅳ. Demand-supply lapse

The four-year cycle of college education cannot (10)_____ rapid changes in market needs.

(6)_____
(7)_____
(8)_____
(9)_____
(10)_____

Mini-Lecture 13

The Sense of Touch

Without looking, you had to (1)_____ how far the door was open and to know when to stop (2)_____ once you'd finished closing the door.

Ⅰ. How does it feel?

Touch turns out extremely (3)_____.

A better understanding of the sense of touch could lead to (4)_____ in medicine, space exploration, robot science, and even video games.

Ⅱ. The healing touch

Visual systems that allow people to work remotely already exist but they have flaws.

To fillone flaw, the scientists are adding a sense of touch to a robot surgical device called the (5)_____.

They have also developed a (6)_____ for the device.

Ⅲ. Pushing paper

Webster's device includes a ball connected to (7)_____.

(1)_____
(2)_____
(3)_____
(4)_____
(5)_____
(6)_____
(7)_____

By sensing small changes in how strongly something is pushed, this type of device could eventually give robots the ability to (8) _____ delicate objects. IV. Touching the future For now, one of (9) _____ of touch technology is how quickly computers can process data. There's also a lot to learn about touch itself. Touch, though very (10) _____, is not quite perfect.	(8) _____ (9) _____ (10) _____

Mini-Lecture 14

Maintain a Healthy Relationship with Your Parents Loving your parents is (1) _____. Here are some healthy ways to forge (2) _____ with your parents. I. Think of them as fellow adults Feeling and acting like an adult around your parents is (3) _____ having an adult relationship with them. II. Talk to your parents as friends A good start is to (4) _____ with your parents on those you have with friends. III. Keep your sense of humor 1) Tell a few jokes. 2) Share some (5) _____ with them 3) Watch the TV show together. IV. Tell your parents your bother 1) Don't be annoyed silently. 2) (6) _____, with gentleness and respect. V. Create opportunities for exploring memories Help our parents (7) _____ in their lives by encouraging them to talk about their stories. VI. Express your appreciation for your parents Your parents still do things for you that deserve your (8) _____.	(1) _____ (2) _____ (3) _____ (4) _____ (5) _____ (6) _____ (7) _____ (8) _____

VII. Rediscover and share mutual interests

Make happy memories the (9) _____ for new and shared activities.

VIII. Look for common activities

Sharing a common task or activity is a great way to (10) _____.

(9) _____

(10) _____

Mini-Lecture 15

The Top Five Things New Musicians Struggle with

As entering the world of music, every musician struggles with certain things. Everyone faces these struggles.

I. Not knowing how to practice

1) (1) _____ practice makes perfect.

2) If you practice something (2) _____, you learn the incorrect way to do it.

II. Lack of an understanding of music

1) Understanding music allows you to understand the (3) _____ and why some sound good together and others don't.

2) Your growth in your musical skill will be (4) _____.

III. Listening to friends and not critics

1) No one ever becomes great without being (5) _____.

2) They don't make fun of but giving you an honest (6) _____ of what they hear.

IV. Unreal expectations

A lot of new musicians want to be able to play the music that attracted them to music (7) _____ and can get very (8) _____ when they can't play it well or quickly.

V. Lack of confidence

1) Lack of confidence causes poor technique and (9) _____ playing, which leads to poor performance.

2) It's one of the most common struggles for musicians and one of (10) _____ to overcome.

(1) _____

(2) _____

(3) _____

(4) _____

(5) _____

(6) _____

(7) _____

(8) _____

(9) _____

(10) _____

203

Mini-Lecture 16

Online Friendship Platforms

Online friendship platforms are experiencing (1)_____. The appearance of Facebook, Twitter, MySpace, LinkedIn, and more causes the (2)_____ of users. Here's a list of the popular sites for making friends online.

Ⅰ. Facebook

1) It is (3)_____ to interested users who register an account.

2) With it, you can set your profile in public or (4)_____.

Ⅱ. MySpace

1) It is also free and comes with (5)_____.

2) It provides a (6)_____ for those who sign up for their service.

Ⅲ. LinkedIn

1) It is a website that allows one to form professional friendships beginning as business friendships but can also transforming into personal "(7)_____" friendships.

2) With it, you build relationships with people who indeed can become lasting friends on a (8)_____ level.

Ⅳ. Twitter

1) You can type only (9)_____ characters in the text box to let others know what you're doing.

2) You connect with people that have (10)_____.

(1)_____
(2)_____
(3)_____
(4)_____
(5)_____
(6)_____
(7)_____
(8)_____
(9)_____
(10)_____

Part Six
Movie Clip Dubbing

Movie Clip

Scar:	Life's not fair, is it? You see I...Well, I shall never be king. And you shall never see the light of another day. Adieu.
Zazu:	Didn't your mother ever tell you not to play with your food?
Scar:	What do you want?
Zazu:	I'm here to announce that King Mufasa is on his way. So you'd better have a good excuse for missing the ceremony this morning.
Scar:	Oh now look Zazu, you made me lose my lunch.
Zazu:	Hah! You'll lose more than that when the king gets through with you. He's as mad as a Hippo with a Hernia.
Scar:	Oh...I quiver with FEAR!
Zazu:	Now Scar, don't look at me that way...HELP!!!!

Mufasa:	Scar!... Drop him.
Scar:	Mmm-Mmm-Hmmm?
Zazu:	Impeccable timing your majesty.
Scar:	Why, if it isn't my big brother descending from on high to mingle with the commoners.
Mufasa:	Sarabi and I didn't see you at the presentation of Simba.
Scar:	That was today? Oh, I feel simply awful. Must have slipped my mind.
Zazu:	Yes, well, as slippery as your mind is, as the king's brother, you should have been first in line!
Scar:	Well, I was first in line...until the little hairball was born.
Mufasa:	That hairball is my son...and your future king.
Scar:	Oh, I shall practice my curtsy.
Mufasa:	Don't turn your back on me, Scar.
Scar:	On, no, Mufasa. Perhaps you shouldn't turn your back on me.
Mufasa:	Is that a challenge?
Scar:	Temper, temper. I wouldn't dream of challenging you.
Zazu:	Pity! Why not?
Scar:	Well, as far as brains go, I got the lion's share. But, when it comes to brute strength, I'm afraid I'm at the shallow end of the gene pool.
Zazu:	There's one in every family, sire. Two in mine, actually. And they always manage to ruin special occasions.
Mufasa:	What am I going to do with him?
Zazu:	He'd make a very handsome throw rug.
Mufasa:	Zazu!
Zazu:	And just think! Whenever he gets dirty, you could take him out and beat him.

Rafiki:	Hmmm...heh heh heh...Simba.
Simba:	Dad! Dad! Come on Dad, we gotta go. Wake up! Oops! Sorry. Dad? Dad. Dad, Dad, Dad, Dad, Dad...
Sarabi:	Your son...is awake...
Mufasa:	Before sunrise, he's your son.
Simba:	Dad. Come on Dad.
Simba:	You Promised!
Mufasa:	Okay, okay. I'm up. I'm up.
Simba:	Yeah!
Mufasa:	Look Simba. Everything the light touches is our kingdom.
Simba:	Wow.
Mufasa:	A king's time as ruler rises and falls like the sun. One day, Simba, the sun will set on my time here and will rise with you as the new king.
Simba:	And this will all be mine?
Mufasa:	Everything.
Simba:	Everything the light touches. What about that shadowy place?
Mufasa:	That's beyond our borders. You must never go there, Simba.
Simba:	But I thought a king could do whatever he wants.
Mufasa:	Oh, there's more to being king than getting your way all the time.
Simba:	There's more?
Mufasa:	Haha. Simba. Everything you see exists together in a delicate balance. As king, you need to understand that balance, and respect all the creatures, from the crawling ant to the leaping antelope.
Simba:	But Dad, don't we eat the antelope?
Mufasa:	Yes, Simba, but let me explain. When we die, our bodies become the grass. And the antelope eat the grass. And so we are all connected in the great circle of life.

Zazu:	Good morning, sire!
Mufasa:	Good morning, Zazu.
Zazu:	Checking in with the morning report.
Mufasa:	Fire away.

Notes

This movie clip is an excerpt from *The Lion King*.

Movie Clip 2

Scene 1	
Princess:	I hate this nightgown. I hate all my night gowns, and I hate all my underwear, too.
Countess:	My dear, you have lovely things.
Princess:	But I'm not two hundred years old. Why can't I sleep in pajamas?
Countess:	Pajamas?
Princess:	Just the top part. Did you know there are people who sleep with absolutely nothing on at all?
Countess:	I rejoice to say that I did not.
Princess:	Listen.
Countess:	Ann, your slippers. Please put on your slippers and come away from the window. Your milk and crackers.
Princess:	Everything we do is so wholesome.
Countess:	They'll help you to sleep.
Princess:	I'm too tired to sleep. I shan't sleep a wink.

Countess:	Now, my dear, if you don't mind, tomorrow's schedule, or "schedule", whichever you prefer. Both are correct. 8:30, breakfast here with the embassy staff. 9:00, we leave for the Polinari automotive works where you'll be presented with a small car.
Princess:	Thank you.
Countess:	Which you will not accept.
Princess:	No, thank you.
Countess:	10:35, inspection of food and agriculturalorganization will present you with an olive tree.
Princess:	No, thank you.
Countess:	Which you will accept.
Princess:	Thank you.
Countess:	10:45, the New Foundling Home for Orphans. You will preside over the laying of the cornerstone. Same speech as last Monday.
Princess:	Trade relations.
Countess:	Yes.
Princess:	For the orphans?
Countess:	No, no, no, the other one.
Princess:	Youth and progress.
Countess:	Precisely. 11:45, back here to rest. No, that's wrong. 11:45, conference here with the press.
Princess:	Sweetness and decency.
Countess:	1:00 sharp, lunch with the Foreign Ministry. You will wear your white lace and carry a bouquet of very small pink roses. 3:05, presentation of a plaque.
Princess:	Thank you.
Countess:	4:10, review Special Guard of Carabinieri.
Princess:	No, thank you.

Countess:	4:45, back here to change into your uniform to meet the...
Princess:	Stop! Stop, stop!
Scene 2	
Princess:	Stop at the next corner, please.
Joe:	OK. Here?
Princess:	Yes. I have to leave you now. I'm going to that corner there and turn. You must stay in the car and drive away. Promise not to watch me go beyond the corner. Just drive away and leave me as I leave you.
Joe:	All right.
Princess:	I don't know how to say good-bye. I can't think of any words.
Joe:	Don't try.
General:	Your Royal Highness. 24 hours, they can't all be blank.
Princess:	They are not.
General:	But what explanation am I to offer Their Majesties?
Princess:	I was indisposed. I am better.
General:	Ma'am, you must appreciate that I have my duty to perform just as Your Royal Highness has her duty.
Princess:	Your Excellency, I trust you will not find it necessary to use that word again. Were I not completely aware of my duty to my family and my country, I would not have come back tonight, or, indeed, ever again. And now, since I understand we have a very full schedule today, you have my permission to withdraw. No milk and crackers. That will be all, thank you, Countess.
Scene 3	
Official:	Ladies and gentlemen, please approach. Her Royal Highness. Your Royal Highness, the ladies and gentlemen of the press. Ladies and gentlemen, Her Royal Highness will now answer your questions.
Journalist 1:	I believe at the outset, Your Highness, that I should express the pleasure of all of us at your recovery from the recent illness.
Princess:	Thank you.

Part Six Movie Clip Dubbing

Journalist 2:	Does Your Highness believe that federation would be a possible solution to Europe's economic problems?
Princess:	I am in favor of any measure which would lead to closer cooperation in Europe.
Journalist 3:	And what, in the opinion of Your Highness, is the outlook for friendship among nations?
Princess:	I have every faith in it, as I have faith in relations between people.
Joe:	May I say, speaking for my own press service, we believe that Your Highness' faith will not be unjustified.
Princess:	I'm so glad to hear you say it.
Journalist 4:	Which of the cities visited did Your Highness enjoy the most?
Princess:	Each in its own way was unforgettable. It would be difficult to... Rome. By all means, Rome. I will cherish my visit here in memory as long as I live.
Journalist 4:	Despite your indisposition, Your Highness?
Princess:	Despite that.

Notes

1. This movie clip is an excerpt from *Roman Holiday*.
2. The princess is addressed as Your Royal Highness.

Movie Clip

Darcy:	Miss Elizabeth. I have struggled in vain and can bear it no longer. These past months have been a torment. I came to Rosings with the single object of seeing you. I had to see you. I have fought against my better judgement, my family's expectation, the inferiority of your birth, my rank and circumstance, all these things, and I'm willing to put them aside and ask you to end my agony.

Elizabeth:	I don't understand.
Darcy:	I love you. Most ardently. Please do me the honour of accepting my hand.
Elizabeth:	Sir, I appreciate the struggle you have been through, and I am very sorry to have caused you pain. Believe me, it was unconsciously done.
Darcy:	Is this your reply?
Elizabeth:	Yes, sir.
Darcy:	Are you laughing at me?
Elizabeth:	No.
Darcy:	Are you rejecting me?
Elizabeth:	I'm sure the feelings which, as you've told me have hindered your regard will help you in overcoming it.
Darcy:	Might I ask why, with so little endeavor at civility, I am thus repulsed?
Elizabeth:	And I might as well inquire why, with so evident a design of insulting me, you chose to tell me you liked me against your better judgement.
Darcy:	No, believe me.
Elizabeth:	If I was uncivil, then that is some excuse! But I have other reasons. You know I have.
Darcy:	What reasons?
Elizabeth:	Do you think that anything might tempt me to accept the man who has ruined, perhaps forever, the happiness of a most beloved sister? Do you deny it, Mr. Darcy? That you separated a young couple who loved each other, exposing your friend to the center of the world for caprice and my sister to its derision for disappointed hopes, and involving them both in misery of the acutest kind?
Darcy:	I do not deny it.

Part Six Movie Clip Dubbing

Elizabeth:	How could you do it?
Darcy:	Because I believed your sister indifferent to him.
Elizabeth:	Indifferent?
Darcy:	I watched them most carefully and realize his attachment was deeper than hers.
Elizabeth:	That's because she's shy.
Darcy:	Bingley, too, is modest and persuaded she didn't feel strongly for him.
Elizabeth:	Because you suggested it.
Darcy:	I did it for his own good.
Elizabeth:	My sister hardly shows her true feelings to me. I suppose you suspect that his fortune had some bearing.
Darcy:	No, I wouldn't do your sister the dishonor! Though it was suggested...
Elizabeth:	What was?
Darcy:	It was made perfectly clear that an advantageous marriage.
Elizabeth:	Did my sister give that impression?
Darcy:	No! No! No! There was, however, I have to admit, the matter of your family.
Elizabeth:	Our want of connection? Mr. Bingley didn't seem to vex himself about that.
Darcy:	No, it was more than that.
Elizabeth:	How, sir?
Darcy:	It was the lack of propriety shown by your mother, your three younger sisters, even, on occasion, your father. Forgive me. You and your sister I must exclude from this.
Elizabeth:	And what about Mr. Wickham?
Darcy:	Mr. Wickham?

Elizabeth:	What excuse can you give for your behavior towards him?
Darcy:	You take an eager interest in that gentleman's concerns.
Elizabeth:	He told me of his misfortunes.
Darcy:	Oh, his misfortunes have been very great indeed.
Elizabeth:	You ruin his chances, and yet you treat him with sarcasm.
Darcy:	So this is your opinion of me? Thank you for explaining so fully. Perhaps these offences might have been overlooked, had not your pride been hurt by my honesty in admitting scruples about our relationship.
Elizabeth:	My pride?
Darcy:	Could you expect me to rejoice in the inferiority of your circumstances?
Elizabeth:	And those are the words of a gentleman. From the first moment I met you, your arrogance and conceit, your selfish disdain for the feelings of others, made me realize you were the last man in the world I could ever be prevailed upon to marry.
Darcy:	Forgive me, madam, for taking up so much of your time.

Notes

This movie clip is an excerpt from *Pride and Prejudice*.

Movie Clip 4

Scene 1	
Forrest:	Hello. My name's Forrest. Forrest Gump. Do you want a chocolate? I could eat about a million and a half of these. My mama always said life was like a box of chocolates. You never know what you're gonna get. Those must be comfortable shoes. I'll bet you could walk all day in shoes like that and not feel a thing. I wish I had shoes like that.

Stranger:	My feet hurt.
Forrest:	Mama always said there's an awful lot you could tell about a person by their shoes: Where they're going, where they've been. I've worn lots of shoes. I bet if I think about it real hard, I could remember my first pair of shoes. Mama said they'd take me anywhere. She said they was my magic shoes.
Doctor:	All right, Forrest, you can open your eyes now. Let's take a little walk around. How do those feel? His legs are strong, Mrs. Gump, as strong as I've ever seen, but his back is as crooked as a politician. But we're gonna straighten him right up, now, aren't we, Forrest?
Mrs. Gump:	Forrest!
Forrest:	Now, when I was a baby, Mama named me after the great Civil War hero, General Nathan Bedford Forrest. She said we was related to him in some way. And what he did was, he started up this club called the Ku Klux Klan. They'd all dress up in their robes and their bed sheets and act like a bunch of ghosts or spooks or something. They'd even put bed sheets on their horses and ride around. And anyway, that's how I got my name, Forrest Gump. Mama said that the "Forrest" part was to remind me that sometimes we all do things that, well, just don't make no sense.
Mrs. Gump:	Okay... Get it, get it... Wait, is it this way? Hold on. All right... What are you all staring at? Haven't you ever seen a little boy with braces on his legs before? Don't ever let anybody tell you they're better than you, Forrest. If God intended everybody to be the same, he'd have given us all braces on our legs.
Forrest:	Mama always had a way of explaining things so I could understand them. We lived about a quarter mile off Route 17, about a half mile from the town of Greenbow, Alabama. That's in the county of Greenbow. Our house had been in Mama's family since her grandpa's grandpa's grandpa had come across the ocean about 1,000 years ago, something like that. Since it was just me and Mama and we had all these empty rooms, Mama decided to let those rooms out, mostly to people passing through, like from, oh, Mobile, Montgomery, places like that. That's how me and Mama got money. Mama was a real smart lady.

Mrs. Gump:	Remember what I told you, Forrest. You're no different than anybody else is. Did you hear what I said, Forrest? You're the same as everybody else. You are no different.

Scene 2

Forrest:	And one day, out of the blue clear sky, I got a letter from Jenny, wondering if I could come down to Savannah and see her, and that's what I'm doing here. She saw me on TV, running. I'm supposed to go on the number 9 bus to Richmond street, and get off and go one block left to 1947 Henry Street, Apartment 4.
Stranger:	Why, you don't need to take a bus. Henry Street is just five or six blocks down that way.
Forrest:	Down that way?
Stranger:	Down that way.
Forrest:	It was nice talking to you.
Stranger:	I hope everything works out for you.
Jenny:	Hey! Forrest! How you doing? Come in, come in!
Forrest:	I got your letter.
Jenny:	I was wondering about that.
Forrest:	Is this your house?
Jenny:	Yeah, it's messy right now. I just got off work.
Forrest:	It's nice. You got air conditioning.
Jenny:	Thank you.
Forrest:	I ate some.
Jenny:	Hey, I kept a scrapbook of your clippings and everything. There you are. And this, I got you running.
Forrest:	I ran a long way, for a long time.
Jenny:	And there...Listen, Forrest, I don't know how to say this. I just I want to apologize for anything that I ever did to you, 'cause I was messed up for a long time, and...

Friend:	(Knocking at door) Yoo-hoo. Hey.
Jenny:	Hey, you. This is an old friend from Alabama.
Friend:	How do you do?
Jenny:	Listen, next week, my schedule changes, so I'll be able to... But thanks.
Friend:	No problem. Got to go, Jan, I'm double-parked.
Jenny:	Okay. Thanks. Bye. This is my very good friend, Mr. Gump. Can you say hi to him?
Forrest Junior:	Hello, Mr. Gump.
Forrest:	Hello.
Forrest Junior:	Can I go watch TV now?
Jenny:	Yes, you can. Just keep it low.
Forrest:	You're a mama, Jenny.
Jenny:	I'm a mama. His name is Forrest.
Forrest:	Like me.
Jenny:	I named him after his daddy.
Forrest:	He got a daddy named Forrest, too?
Jenny:	You're his daddy, Forrest.

Notes

1. This movie clip is an excerpt from *Forrest Gump*.
2. Ku Klux Klan is a secret organization of white men in the southern states of the US who use violence to oppose social change and equal rights for black people.

Movie Clip

Juliana:	I see why you like to come out here.
Dad:	Would you mind explaining it to your mother?

Narrator:	I love to watch my father paint. Oh, really, I love to hear him talk while he painted. I learned a lot about my dad that day. He told me all sorts of things, like how he got his first job delivering hay and how he'd wished he'd finished college. Then one day he surprised me.
Dad:	What's going on with you and, uh, Bryce Loski?
Juliana:	What do you mean? Nothing.
Dad:	Oh, okay. My mistake.
Juliana:	Why would you even think that?
Dad:	No reason. Just that you talk about him all the time.
Juliana:	I do?
Dad:	Uh, hum.
Juliana:	I don't know. I guess it's something about his eyes. Or maybe his smile.
Dad:	But what about him?
Juliana:	What?
Dad:	You have to look at the whole landscape.
Juliana:	What does that mean?
Dad:	A painting is more than the sum of its parts. A cow by itself is just a cow. A meadow by itself is just grass, flowers. And the sun peeking through the trees is just a beam of light. But you put them all together, and it can be magic.
Narrator:	I didn't really understand what he was saying until one afternoon, when I was up in the sycamore tree. I was rescuing a kite. It was a long way up, higher than I'd ever been. And the higher I got, the more amazed I was by the view. I began to notice how wonderful the breeze smelled. Like sunshine and wild grass. I couldn't stop breathing it in, filling my lungs with sweetness smell I'd ever known.
Bryce:	Hey, you found my kite.
Juliana:	Bryce, you should come up here. It's so beautiful.

Bryce:	I can't. I sprained mine, um, I have a rash.
Narrator:	From that moment on, that became my spot. I could sit there for hours, just looking out at the world. Some days the sunsets would be purple and pink. And some days they were blazing orange, setting fire to the clouds on the horizon. It was during one of those sunsets that my father's idea of the whole being greater than the sum of its parts moved from my head to my heart. Some days I would get there extra early to watch the sunrise. One morning I was making mental notes of how the streaks of light were cutting through the clouds, so I could tell my dad when I heard a noise below.
Juliana:	Excuse me. Excuse me. I'm sorry, but you can't park there. That's the bus stop.
Tree Worker 1:	Hey, what are you doing up there?
Tree Worker 2:	You can't be up there. We're gonna take this thing down.
Juliana:	The tree?
Tree Worker 1:	Yeah. Now come on down.
Juliana:	But who told you, you could cut it down?
Tree Worker 2:	The owner.
Juliana:	Why?
Tree Worker 2:	He's gonna build a house, and this tree's in the way. So come on, girl, we got work to do.
Juliana:	You can't cut down. You just can't.
Tree Worker 2:	Listen, girl, I'm this close to calling the police. You are trespassing and obstructing progress on a contracted job. Now either you come down or we're gonna cut you down.
Juliana:	Go ahead. Cut it down. I'm not coming down. I'm never coming down. Bryce. You guys, come up here with me. They won't cut it down if we're all up here. Bryce, please don't let them do this. Come on, you guys. Bryce, please. You don't have to come up this high. Just a little ways. Bryce, please, please.

Narrator:	What happened after that was a blur. It seemed like the whole town was there. But still I wouldn't move. Then my father showed up. He talked a fireman into letting him come up to where I was.
Dad:	Sweetie, it's time to come down.
Juliana:	Daddy, please don't let them do this.
Dad:	Sweetie.
Juliana:	Daddy, look, you can see everything. You can see the whole world from here.
Dad:	No view is worth my daughter's safety. Now, come on.
Juliana:	I can't.
Dad:	Juliana, it's time to come down now.
Juliana:	Please, daddy.
Dad:	It's time.
Narrator:	And that was it. I must've cried for two weeks straight. Oh, sure, I went to school and did the best I could, but nothing seemed to matter.

This movie clip is an excerpt from *Flipped*.

Movie Clip

Mr. Ping:	You know, you weren't the only one who was lying. I didn't really come along because I was worried Po would go hungry. I was worried about you.
Li Shan:	Worried that I'd go hungry?

Mr. Ping:	No, I was worried you'd steal Po from me.
Li Shan:	I'd what?
Mr. Ping:	I know. That was crazy. But I realized having you in Po's life doesn't mean less for me. It means more for Po.
Li Shan:	Oh. Well, I'm not in his life. Not anymore.
Mr. Ping:	Your son got mad at you. Welcome to parenthood.
Li Shan:	You don't understand. I lied to him. He'll never forgive me.
Mr. Ping:	I lied to him for 20 years. He still thinks he came from an egg. Sometimes we do the wrong things for the right reasons. Look, he's hurt. He's confused and he still has to save the world. He needs both his dads.
Tigress:	This isn't going to work.
Po:	It has to.
Tigress:	You're not thinking straight.
Po:	I am.
Tigress:	You're not.
Po:	I am.
Tigress:	No.
Po:	Yes, I am.
Tigress:	No, I've seen Kai. I see what he can do.
Po:	But he hasn't seen what I can do.
Tigress:	The Wuxi Finger Hold?
Po:	That's my best move. I just have to get to Kai, grab his finger, and then, Skadoosh, back to the spirit realm.
Tigress:	He has an army of jade warriors. Everything they see, he sees. So, there's no sneaking up on him. You'll never get close enough.
Po:	It's gonna work.
Tigress:	He can only be stopped by a master of chi.

Po:	Oh, you sound just like Shifu with the chi, chi, chi. Chi this, chi that. Chi, chi, chi, chi. I'm not a Master of chi, OK? I don't know if I'm the Dragon Warrior. I don't even know if I'm a panda. I don't know who I am. You are right. There's no way I can stop him and his army.
Li Shan:	Unless you had an army of your own.
Po:	You?
Li Shan:	Not just me.
Mr. Ping:	Us.
Li Shan:	All of us. I finally found my son after all these years. It's gonna take a lot more than the end of the world to keep us apart.
Po:	But you don't even know kung fu.
Li Shan:	Then you will teach us.
Po:	What? I can't teach you kung fu. I couldn't even teach Tigress. And she already knows kung fu!
Li Shan:	Po, I know. I'm the last guy you wanna trust right now. But you gotta believe me. We can do this. We can learn kung fu. We can be just like you.
Po:	What did you just say?
Li Shan:	Ur... We can do this?
Po:	No.
Li Shan:	We can learn kung fu?
Po:	After that.
Li Shan:	Ur... I... We can be just like you?
Po:	Yes!
Li Shan:	We can?
Po:	No, you can't. But you don't have to be. That's what Shifu meant. I don't have to turn you into me. I have to turn you into you!

Part Six Movie Clip Dubbing

Mr. Ping:	That doesn't make any sense.
Po:	I know. Thanks, dads.
Mr. Ping & Li Shan:	You're welcome?
Po:	I'm gonna do something I never thought I'd be able to do. I'm gonna teach kung fu. You guys, your real strength comes from being the best you can be. So who are you? What are you good at? What do you love? What makes you you? Yes, good, good, again. Good, again. Good, good, good, again.

 Notes

This movie clip is an excerpt from *Kung Fu Panda* 3.

Movie Clip

Annie:	How far away is your home?
Hallie:	Oh, California is way at the other end of the country. Actually, here's a picture of my house.
Annie:	Wow! It's beautiful.
Hallie:	Yeah. We built it when I was little. We've got this incredible porch that looks over the entire vineyard, and then—
Annie:	Who...who's that?
Hallie:	Oh, that's my dad. He didn't know I was taking the picture then, or else he would have turned around. He's kinda like my best friend. We do everything together. What's the matter?

223

Annie:	Oh. It's chilling here. That's all.
Hallie:	Want one?
Annie:	Oh, sure. I love Oreos. At home I eat them with... I eat them with peanut butter.
Hallie:	You do? That is so weird. So do I.
Annie:	You're kidding. Most people find that totally disgusting.
Hallie:	I know. I don't get it.
Annie:	Me either.
Hallie:	What's your dad like? I mean, is he the kind of father you can talk to, or is he one of those workaholic types who says, "I'll talk to ya later, honey...", but you know, never really does? I hate that!
Annie:	I don't have a father, actually. I mean, I had one once, I suppose... But my parents divorced years ago. My mother never even mentions him. It's like he evaporated into thin air, or something...
Hallie:	It's scary the way nobody stays together anymore.
Annie:	Tell me about it.
Hallie:	How old are you?
Annie:	I'll be 12 on October 11.
Hallie:	So will I.
Annie:	Your birthday's on October 11?
Hallie:	Yeah.
Annie:	How weird is that?
Hallie:	Extremely. It stopped raining. You wanna go get a popsicle or something? What's the matter?
Annie:	Hallie, what's your mother like?
Hallie:	I never met her. She and my dad split up when I was a baby, maybe even before. I'm not sure. He doesn't like to talk about her. But I know she was really, really beautiful.

Annie:	How do you know that?
Hallie:	Well, because my dad had this old picture of her hidden in his sock drawer, and he caught me looking at it like all the time, so he gave it to me to keep. Look, I'm... I'm really thirsty. Sure, you don't want to go to the mess hall and get lemonade?
Annie:	Will you stop thinking about your stomach at a time like this?
Hallie:	At a time like what?
Annie:	Don't you realize what's happening? I mean, think about it. I only have a mother, and you only have a father. You've never seen your mom, and I've never seen my dad. You have one old picture of your mom and I have one old picture of my dad. At least yours is probably a whole picture. Mine is a pathetic little thing, all crinkled and ripped right down the middle and... What are you rummaging in your trunk for?
Hallie:	This. It's a picture of my mom and it's ripped, too.
Annie:	Right down the middle?
Hallie:	Right down the middle.
Annie:	This is so... freaky. On the count of three, we'll show them to each other, okay?
Hallie:	Okay.
Annie & Hallie:	1, 2, 3.
Hallie:	That's my dad.
Annie:	That's my mom. That's the lunch bell.
Hallie:	I'm not so hungry anymore. So, if your mom is my mom, and my dad is your dad, and we're both born on October 11, then you and I are like... like sisters.
Annie:	Sisters? Hallie, we're like twins!

Notes

This movie clip is an excerpt from *The Parent Trap*.

Movie Clip

Andy:	Hi. Uh, I have an appointment with Emily Charlton?
Emily:	Andy Sachs?
Andy:	Yes.
Emily:	Great. Human Resources certainly has an odd sense of humor. Follow me. Okay, so I was Miranda's second assistant... but her first assistant recently got promoted, and so now I'm the first.
Andy:	Oh, and you're replacing yourself.
Emily:	Well, I am trying. Miranda sacked the last two girls after only a few weeks. We need to find someone who can survive here. Do you understand?
Andy:	Yeah. Of course. Who's Miranda?
Emily:	Oh, my God. I will pretend you did not just ask me that. She's the editor in chief of *Runway*, not to mention a legend. You work a year for her, and you can get a job at any magazine you want. A million girls would kill for this job.
Andy:	It sounds like a great opportunity. I'd love to be considered.
Emily:	Andrea, *Runway* is a fashion magazine, so an interest in fashion is crucial.
Andy:	What makes you think I'm not interested in fashion?
Emily:	Oh, my God. No! No! No!

Andy:	What's wrong?
Emily:	She's on her way. Tell everyone!
Nigel:	She's not supposed to be here until 9:00.
Emily:	Her driver just text-messaged and her facialist ruptured a disk. God, these people!
Nigel:	Who's that?
Emily:	That I can't even talk about.
Nigel:	All right, everyone! Gird your loins[2]! Did somebody eat an onion bagel?
Model:	Sorry, Miranda.
Emily:	Move it! Ooh!
Miranda:	I don't understand why it's so difficult to confirm an appointment.
Emily:	I know. I'm so sorry, Miranda. I actually did confirm last night.
Miranda:	Details of your incompetence do not interest me. Tell Simone I'm not going to approve that girl that she sent me for the Brazilian layout. I asked for clean, athletic, smiling. She sent me dirty, tired and paunchy. And R.S.V.P. Yes to Michael Kors' party. I want the driver to drop me off at 9:30 and pick me up at 9:45 sharp. Call Natalie at Glorious Foods, tell her no for the 40th time. No! I don't want dacquoise. I want tortes filled with warm rhubarb compote. Then call my ex-husband and remind him the parent-teacher conference is at Dalton tonight. Then call my husband, ask him to meet me for dinner at that place I went to with Massimo. Tell Richard I saw the pictures that he sent for that feature on the female paratroopers and they're all so deeply unattractive. Is it impossible to find a lovely, slender, female paratrooper?
Emily:	No.
Miranda:	Am I reaching for the stars here? Not really. Also, I need to see all the things that Nigel has pulled for Gwyneth's second cover try. I wonder if she's lost any of that weight yet. Who's that?

Emily:	Nobody. Oh, um, well, Human Resources sent her up about the new assistant job, and I was sort of "pre-interviewing" her for you, but she's hopeless and totally wrong for it.
Miranda:	Clearly I'm going to have to do that myself because the last two you sent me were completely inadequate. So send her in. That's all.
Emily:	Right. She wants to see you.
Andy:	Oh! She does?
Emily:	Move!
Andy:	This is foul. Don't let her see it. Go! That's...
Miranda:	Who are you?
Andy:	Uh, my name is Andy Sachs. I recently graduated from Northwestern University.
Miranda:	And what are you doing here?
Andy:	Well, I think I could do a good job as your assistant. And, um... Yeah, I came to New York to be a journalist, and I sent out letters out everywhere, and I finally got a call from Elias Clark and met with Sherry up at Human Resources. Basically, it's this or Auto Universe.
Miranda:	So you don't read *Runway*?
Andy:	Uh, no.
Miranda:	And before today, you had never heard of me.
Andy:	No.
Miranda:	And you have no style or sense of fashion.
Andy:	Well, um, I think that depends on what you're...
Miranda:	No, no. That wasn't a question.
Andy:	Um, I was editor in chief of the *Daily Northwestern*. I also, um, won a national competition for college journalists with my series on the janitor's union, which exposed the exploitation...
Miranda:	That's all.

Part Six Movie Clip Dubbing

Andy:	Yeah, you know, okay. You're right. I don't fit in here. I'm not skinny or glamorous, and I don't know that much about fashion, but I'm smart. I learn fast and I will work very hard.
Nigel:	I got the exclusive on the Cavalli for Gwyneth, but the problem is, with that huge feathered headdress that she's wearing, she looks like she's working the main stage at the Golden Nugget.
Andy:	Thank you for your time.

 Notes

1. This movie clip is an excerpt from *The Devil Wears Prada*.
2. Gird your loins: to prepare oneself to face or contend with something.

Part Seven
Theatrical Performance

Drama Clip *Troy*[1]

Odysseus[2]:	Your reputation for hospitality[3] is fast becoming legend.
Achilles[4]:	Patroclus[5], my cousin. Odysseus, king of Ithaca[6].
Odysseus:	Patroclus, I know your parents well. I miss them. Now you have this one watching over[7] you, eh? Learning from Achilles himself. Kings would kill for the honor.
Achilles:	Are you here at Agamemnon[8]'s bidding?
Odysseus:	We need to talk.
Achilles:	I will not fight for him.
Odysseus:	I'm not asking you to fight for him. I'm asking you to fight for the Greeks.
Achilles:	Why? Are the Greeks[9] tired of fighting each other?
Odysseus:	For now.
Patroclus:	For the Greeks.

Part Seven Theatrical Performance

Achilles:	The Trojans[10] never harmed me.
Odysseus:	They insulted Greece.
Achilles:	They insulted one Greek, a man who couldn't hold on to his wife. What business is that of mine?
Odysseus:	Your business is war, my friend.
Achilles:	Is it? Am I the whore of the battlefield? The man has no honor. I won't be remembered as a tyrant's mercenary.
Odysseus:	Let Achilles fight for honor. Let Agamemnon fight for power. And let the gods decide which man to glorify. Forget Agamemnon, fight for me. My wife will feel much better if she knows you're by my side. I'll feel much better... We're sending the largest fleet[11] that ever sailed. A thousand ships.

1. *Troy* was directed by Wolfgang Petersen and was released in 2004, nominated for Oscar Academy Award for Best Achievement in Costume Design in 2005. Brad Pitt, starring Achilles, also won Teen Choice Award for Choice Movie Actor—Drama/Action Adventure, and so did Peter O'Toole, starring Priam, for Best Supporting Actor in Film in Irish Film and Television Award. This film clip is Odysseus comes to talk Achilles into going to the war against Troy. The film *Troy* is inspired by Homer's Greek mythology classic *The ILiad*(《伊利亚特》).

The following words and expressions are related to Greek mythology.

Mount Olympus:奥林匹斯山（希腊神话中众神居住的山）
Muse：缪斯（掌管诗歌、音乐、学问等的女神）
Nymph：宁芙（海神）
Titan：泰坦族（天神与地神所生子女组成的巨人族）
Naiad：那伊阿得（水泉女神）
Zeus：宙斯（奥林匹斯山的主神）
Hera：赫拉（宙斯的妻子）
Apollo：阿波罗（太阳神）

Poseidon：波塞顿（海神）

Athena：雅典娜（智慧女神）

Ares：阿瑞斯（战神）

Artemis：阿耳忒弥斯（狩猎女神）

Aphrodite：阿佛洛狄特（爱与美女神）

Dionysus：狄俄尼索斯（酒神）

Hephaestus：赫菲斯托斯（火与锻冶之神）

Hercules：赫拉克利斯（大力神）

Hermes：赫耳墨斯（掌管商业道路等之神）

Uranus：乌拉诺斯（天神）

Gaea：盖亚（大地女神）

Oedipus：俄狄浦斯

Adonis：阿多尼斯（美少年）

Pandora：潘多拉（人间第一个女人）

Troy：特洛伊

2. Odysseus：奥德修斯（《奥德赛》中的主人公，指挥特洛伊战争，使希腊获胜）

3. hospitality：殷勤款待，好客

4. Achilles：阿喀琉斯（希腊神话中著名的英雄）

5. Patroclus：帕特洛克罗斯（阿喀琉斯好友）

6. Ithaca：伊萨卡岛（希腊西部爱奥尼亚海中群岛之一）

7. watch over：照看

8. Agamemnon：阿伽门农（特洛伊战争中希腊军队的统帅）

9. Greek：希腊人

10. Trojan：特洛伊人

11. fleet：船队

Drama Clip 2 *The Joy Luck Club*[1]

Harold：	What's going on?
Lena：	I don't think you should get credit for[2] your ice cream any more.
Harold：	Fine. You got it. End of discussion[3]!

Lena:	Why do you have to be so goddamn fair?
Harold:	Just what is this about exactly?
Lena:	I don't know. Maybe everything. The way we account for everything. What we share, what we don't share. I'm sick of[4] it. Adding things up[5], subtracting[6]. Making it come out even when it's not. I'm sick of it.
Harold:	You are the one who wanted the cat!
Lena:	What are you talking about?
Harold:	All right. If you think I'm being unfair, we'll both pay for the fleas[7].
Lena:	This is not about fleas. That is not the point.
Harold:	Then, please, tell me, what is the point?
Lena:	I, ju... I just think that we need to change things. We need to think about what this marriage is based on. Not this balance sheet[8].
Harold:	Well, I know what our marriage is based upon. And if you don't, then you'd better think about it before you start to change things.

Notes

1. This is a clip from *The Joy Luck Club*. Lena, inheriting her mother's passivity and obedience, was financially exploited by her husband and showing unreasonable compromise. In this clip, Lena complains to her husband Harold about their constantly keeping separate accounts and sharing very little in domestic life. *The Joy Luck Club* was directed by Wayne Wang and released in 1993. The film was nominated for BAFTA Film Award for Best Screenplay, and Adapted Screenplay. *The Joy Luck Club* consists of four stories about generational and cultural clashes and communications between immigrant mothers and their American-born daughters.

2. get credit for: 因……受到赞誉

3. end of discussion: 讨论结束

4. be sick of: 厌倦

5. add up：合计；相加

6. subtract：减去；扣除

7. flea：跳蚤

8. not this balance sheet：不是这个资产负债表

Drama Clip *The Pursuit of Happyness*[1]

Secretary：	Chris Gardner.
Chris：	Chris Gardner. How are you? Good morning. Chris Gardner. Chris Gardner. Good to see you again. Chris Gardner. Pleasure. I've been sitting out there for the last half-hour trying to come up with a story[2] that would explain my being here dressed like this[3]. And I wanted to come up with a story that would demonstrate[4] qualities that I'm sure you all admire[5] here, like earnestness[6] or diligence[7], team-playing[8], something. And I couldn't think of anything. So the truth is... I was arrested[9] for failure to pay parking tickets[10].
Frohm：	Parking tickets?
Chris：	And I ran all the way here from the police station[11].
Frohm：	What were you doing before you were arrested?
Chris：	I was painting my apartment.
Twistle：	He's been waiting outside the front of the building... with some 40-pound gizmo[12] for over a month.
Frohm：	He said you're smart.
Chris：	Well, I'd like to think so.
Frohm：	And you want to learn this business?
Chris：	Yes, sir, I wanna learn this business.
Frohm：	Have you already started learning on your own[13]?
Chris：	Absolutely.

Part Seven　Theatrical Performance

Frohm：	Jay?
Twistle：	Yes, sir.
Frohm：	How many times have you seen Chris?
Twistle：	I don't know. One too many, apparently.
Chris：	Was he ever dressed like this?
Twistle：	No. No. Jacket and tie.
Frohm：	First in your class? In school? High school?
Chris：	Yes, sir.
Frohm：	How many in the class?
Chris：	Twelve. It was a small town.
Frohm：	I'll say.
Chris：	But I was also first in my radar class in the Navy, and that was a class of 20... Can I say something? I'm the type of person... if you ask me a question and I don't know the answer I'm gonna tell you that I don't know. But I bet you what, I know how to find the answer, and I will find the answer. Is that fair enough?
Frohm：	Chris, what would you say if a guy walked in for an interview without a shirt on... and I hired him? What would you say?
Chris：	He must've had on some really nice pants.

1. This clip is from *The Pursuit of Happyness*, which tells us a story of a struggling salesman taking custody of his son as he's poised to begin a life-changing professional career. Notice the name of the film, *The Pursuit of Happyness*, which is deliberately misspelled. There is an I in "happiness". There is no Y (why) in "happiness".

2. come up with a story：编出个理由

3. explain my being here dressed like this：解释我这身打扮出现的原因

4. demonstrate qualities：证明（优秀）品质

5. admire：赞赏

6. earnestness：诚挚

7. diligence：勤奋

8. team-playing：团队合作

9. arrest：逮捕

10. parking ticket：违章停车罚单

11. And I ran all the way here from the polk station, the police station. 我是从警差局……警察局一路跑来的

12. gizmo：小装置；小玩意儿

13. learning on one's own：自学

Drama Clip *Forrest Gump*[1]

Gump：	Since it was just me and Mama and we had all these empty[2] rooms, Mama decided to let those rooms out, mostly to people passing through, like from, oh, Mobile, Montgomery, places like that. That's how me and Mama got money. Mama was a real smart lady.
Mrs. Gump：	Remember what I told you, Forrest. You're no different than anybody else is. Did you hear what I said, Forrest? You are the same as everybody else. You are no different.
Mr. Hancock：	Your boy's...different, Mrs. Gump. His IQ[3] is 75.
Mrs. Gump：	Well, we're all different, Mr. Hancock.
Mr. Hancock：	I want to show you something, Mrs. Gump. Now, this is normal. Forrest is right here. The state requires a minimum IQ of 80 to attend public school. Mrs. Gump, he's going to have to go to a special school. Now, he'll be just fine.
Mrs. Gump：	What does normal mean anyway? He might be... a bit on the slow side, but my boy Forrest is going to get the same opportunities as everyone else. He's not going to some special school to learn how to retread[4] tires. We're talking about five little points here. There must be something can be done.

Part Seven Theatrical Performance

Mr. Hancock:	We're a progressive[5] school system. We don't want to see anybody left behind. Is there a Mr. Gump, Mrs. Gump?
Mrs. Gump:	He's on vacation.

Notes

1. This clip is from *Forrest Gump*. Mrs. Gump was trying to get an opportunity for Forrest Gump to go to a normal school, however Mr. Hancock refused to accept him. *Forrest Gump* (1994) was directed by Robert Zemeckis.

2. empty：空的；无意义的

3. IQ：Intelligence Quotient 智商

4. retread：给（旧车胎）装新胎面

5. progressive：先进的

Drama Clip 5 *The Queen*[1]

Queen:	How nice to see you again, Mr. Blair. And congratulations!
Blair:	Thank you.
Queen:	Your children must be very proud.
Blair:	I hope so.
Queen:	You've three, haven't you?
Blair:	That's right.
Queen:	How lovely! Such a blessing[2], children. Please, do sit down.
Blair:	Thank you.
Queen:	Have we shown you how to start a nuclear war yet?
Blair:	Er...no.
Queen:	Oh. First thing we do, apparently, then we take away your passport and spend the rest of the time sending you around the world.

Blair:	You obviously know my job better than I do.
Queen:	Yes, well, you are my tenth prime minister, Mr. Blair. My first, of course, was Winston Churchill. He sat in your chair in a frock coat and top hat. He was kind enough to give a shy young girl like me quite an education.
Blair:	I can imagine.
Queen:	With time, one has hopefully added experience to that education, and a little wisdom, better enabling us to execute our constitutional responsibility, to advise, guide, and warn the government of the day.
Blair:	Advice which I... look forward to receiving.
Queen:	Yes, we'll save that for our weekly meeting. If there's nothing else, I believe we have some business to attend to.
Blair:	Of course. Your Majesty, my party has won the election, so now I come to you to ask your permission to form a government.
Queen:	No, Mr. Blair. Mr. Blair, I ask the question. The duty falls upon me, as your sovereign, to invite you to become Prime Minister, and to form a government in my name... And if you agree, the custom is to say yes.
Blair:	Yes.

1. This clip is from *The Queen*. It tells us that after the death of Princess Diana, Queen Elizabeth Ⅱ struggles with her reaction to a sequence of events nobody could have predicted. Diana, the "People's Princess" has died in a car accident in Paris. The Queen (Dame Helen Mirren) and her family decide that for the best, they should remain hidden behind the closed doors of Balmoral Castle. The heartbroken public do not understand and request that the Queen comforts her people. This also puts pressure on newly elected Tony Blair (Michael Sheen), who constantly tries to convince the monarchy to address the public.

There are expressions related to the British monarchy listed below:
absolute monarchy 君主专制
constitutional monarchy 君主立宪制
His/ Her Majesty (HM) 国王陛下/女王陛下
King 国王
Queen 女王
His / Her Royal Highness (HRH) 殿下
prince 亲王;王子
princess 公主;王妃
queen regnant 执政(当朝)女王
prince consort 女王(或女皇)的丈夫
queen dowager 国王遗孀
queen mother 王太后
the Prince and Princess of Wales 威尔士亲王及王妃
the Princess Royal 长公主
Buckingham Palace 白金汉宫
Windsor Castle 温莎城堡
Balmoral Castle 巴尔莫勒尔城堡
the Royal Coat of Arms 王室纹章
the Civil List 王室年俸
the privy purse (英国国王或女王的)私用金
Windsor protocol 王室礼仪
Royal Standard 王室旗帜
lady of the bedchamber (英国)女王内侍
equerry 英国王室侍从武官
Household Cavalry (英军负责王室警卫工作的)皇家骑兵团
Trooping the Colour 英国皇家军队阅兵仪式
peerage 贵族

2. blessing：幸事;福祉
3. nuclear：原子核的;核武器的
4. prime minister：首相;总理
5. frock：女装;连衣裙
6. top hat：高顶礼帽
7. constitutional：宪法的;合乎宪法的

Drama Clip 6 *The Shawshank Redemption*[1]

Red:	And that's how it came to pass... that on the second-to-last day of the job... the convict crew that tarred[2] the plate factory roof in the spring of '49... wound up[3] sitting in a row at 10:00 in the morning... drinking icy-cold Bohemia style beer, courtesy[4] of the hardest screw... that ever walked a turn at Shawshank State Prison.
Hadley:	Drink up while it's cold, ladies.
Red:	The colossal prick even managed to sound magnanimous. We sat and drank with the sun on our shoulders and felt like free men. Hell, we could have been tarring the roof of one of our own houses. We were the lords of all creation. As for Andy... he spent that break hunkered in the shade... a strange little smile on his face... watching us drink his beer.
Heywood:	Hey. Want a cold one, Andy?
Andy:	No, thanks. I gave up drinking.
Red:	You could argue he'd done it to curry favor with[5] the guards. Or maybe make a few friends among us cons. Me? I think he did it just to feel normal again... if only for a short while.

Notes

1. This clip is from *The Shawshank Redemption*. *The Shawshank Redemption* was a movie about two convicts, who formed a friendship, over the course of several years, seeking consolation and, eventually, redemption through basic compassion.
2. tar: 涂以焦油
3. wind up: (令人意想不到地)以……告终
4. courtesy: 好意;恩惠
5. hunker: 蹲下;盘坐
6. curry favor with: 巴结;拍马屁

Part Seven Theatrical Performance

Drama Clip 7 *Mission Impossible*: III[1]

Baddy:	We've put an explosive[2] charge in your head. Does that sound familiar[3]? The Rabbit's Foot. Where is it?
Ethan:	I gave it to you.
Baddy:	Ethan, where's the Rabbit's Foot?
Ethan:	Wait... What are you saying? That wasn't it? What I gave you, was that...
Baddy:	I'm going to count[4] to 10. You're going to tell me where the Rabbit's Foot is or she dies.
Ethan:	Jules, it's going to be okay. It's going to be okay. Do you understand?
Baddy:	One.
Ethan:	You listen to me. I got exactly[5] what you asked for. Did you want something else? If there was a misunderstanding[6], I will fix[7] it. I can get it, whatever you want.
Baddy:	Two.
Ethan:	Listen. Talk to me. We can talk, like gentlemen.
Baddy:	Three.
Ethan:	God! All right. All right, all right. I know where the Rabbit's Foot is. I can help you.
Baddy:	The way you helped me on the airplane[8]? That way?
Ethan:	You put the gun down. I'm not talking to you like this.
Baddy:	That's your choice. Four.
Ethan:	The Rabbit's Foot's in Paris. You want to know where in Paris? Then let her go. 'Cause you will not...
Baddy:	It's not in Paris. Five.
Ethan:	I can get it for you. But you kill her, you do this, you get nothing.

241

Notes

1. This clip is from *Mission Impossible*: Ⅲ (2006). Actually, the film is a series and followed by more. *Mission Impossible*: Ⅲ tells us that an IMF agent Ethan Hunt comes into conflict with a dangerous and sadistic arms dealer who threatens his life and his fiancée in response.

2. explosive：能引起爆炸的

3. familiar：熟悉的；常见的

4. count：数数

5. exactly：恰好地；正是

6. misunderstanding：误解；误会

7. fix：解决（问题）

8. airplane：飞机

Drama Clip 8 *Zootopia*[1]

Judy：	You're under arrest[2].
Nick：	Really, for what?
Judy：	Gee, I don't know. How about selling food without a permit[3], transporting undeclared commerce[4] across borough lines, false advertising[5]...
Nick：	Permit. Receipt of declared commerce. And I didn't falsely advertise anything. Take care.
Judy：	You told that mouse the Popsicle sticks were redwood!
Nick：	That's right. "Red wood." With a space in the middle. Wood that is red. You can't touch me, Carrots, I've been doing this since I was born.
Judy：	You're gonna wanna refrain[6] from calling me Carrots...

Part Seven　Theatrical Performance

Nick：	My bad. I just naturally assumed[7] you came from some little carrot-choked Podunk. No?
Judy：	Ah, no. Podunk is in Deerbrooke county, and I grew up in Bunnyburrow.
Nick：	Okay. Tell me if this story sounds familiar. Naive[8] little hick with good grades and big ideas decides, "Hey, look at me, I'm gonna move to Zootopia... where predators[9] and prey live in harmony[10] and sing Kumbaya!" Only to find... whoopsie, we don't all get along. And that dream of becoming a big-city cop? Double whoopsie! She's a meter maid. And whoopsie number three-sie, no one cares about her or her dreams. And soon enough those dreams die, and our bunny sinks into emotional[11] and literal squalor,[12] living in a box under a bridge. Till finally she has no choice but to go back home with that cute fuzzy-wuzzy little tail between her legs to become... You're from Bunnyburrow, is that what you said? So how about a carrot farmer? Does that sound about right?
Judy：	Oh...

Notes

1. This clip is from *Zootopia*. It is a story about a rookie bunny cop and a cynical con artist fox working together to uncover a conspiracy in a city of anthropomorphic animals.

2. arrest：逮捕

3. permit：许可证

4. commerce：商业；贸易

5. advertise：做广告

6. refrain：抑制

7. assume：假定；推测

8. naive：天真的

9. predator：食肉动物

10. harmony：和谐的

11. emotional：情感的

12. squalor：肮脏；邋遢

参考文献

[1] Lynn A. Appreciating Cinema[M]. 霍斯亮, 译. 北京: 外语教学与研究出版社, 2005.

[2] 戴祯琼, 丁言仁. 背诵课文在中国学生英语学习中的作用研究[J]. 外语研究, 2010(02): 46-52.

[3] 丁言仁, 戚焱. 背诵课文在英语学习中的作用[J]. 外语界, 2001(05): 58-65.

[4] 丁言仁. 课文背诵与模仿——成功英语学习者的学习经验[J]. 中国外语教育, 2008, 1(02): 19-26, 78-79.

[5] 丰玉芳. 英语专业高低年级学生词汇学习策略比较研究[J]. 外语界, 2003(02): 66-72.

[6] 金国臣. 英语电影赏析[M]. 北京: 清华大学出版社, 2016.

[7] 顾悦. 回归经典阅读: 英语专业的人文性与基于阅读经验的文学教育[J]. 外语教学理论与实践, 2016(02): 42-46.

[8] 刘凌, 秦晓晴. 词汇呈现方式对英语词汇学习影响的实证研究[J]. 外语界, 2014(02): 67-75.

[9] 刘美兰. 从英语戏剧表演看大学生跨文化交际能力的培养[J]. 中山大学学报论丛, 2005(04): 410-413.

[10] 聂龙. 进一步加强词汇教学——论词汇教学的重要性[J]. 外语界, 2001(03): 57-63.

[11] 潘赛仙. 英语电影配音秀在大学英语教学中的作用——一次WebQuest教学模式的尝试[J]. 桂林师范高等专科学校学报, 2013, 27(02): 101-104.

[12] 教育部高等学校教学指导委员会. 普通高等学校本科专业类教学质量国家标准[M]. 北京: 高等教育出版社, 2018.

[13] 教育部高等学校外国语言文学类专业教学指导委员会英语专业教学指导分委员会. 普通高等学校本科外国语言文学类专业教学指南[M]. 北京：外语教学与研究出版社, 2020.

[14] 王红梅. 运用英文电影配音提高大学生英语听说能力教学实践探索[J]. 江苏技术师范学院学报, 2014, 20（01）：105-108.

[15] 吴菲衡, 刘思岳, Marie White. 看电影学英语年度合集（2017版）[M]. 北京：石油工业出版社, 2017.

[16] 习近平. 习近平谈治国理政（第三卷）[M]. 北京：外文出版社, 2020.

[17] 习近平. 习近平谈治国理政（第三卷）（英文版）[M]. 北京：外文出版社, 2020.

[18] 习近平. 习近平谈治国理政（第四卷）[M]. 北京：外文出版社, 2022.

[19] 习近平. 习近平谈治国理政（第四卷）（英文版）[M]. 北京：外文出版社, 2022.

[20] 徐志英, 邓杉, 赵蓉. 英语电影视听说[M]. 北京：外语教学与研究出版社, 2009.

[21] 杨自伍. 英国散文名篇欣赏[M]. 2版. 上海：上海外语教育出版社, 2010.

[22] 杨自伍. 英国文化选本[M]. 2版. 上海：上海外语教育出版社, 2010.

[23] 张兴华, 韩梅, 张兴梅. 英语电影视听说与赏析[M]. 北京：光明日报出版社, 2015.

与本书配套的二维码资源使用说明

　　本书部分课程及与纸质教材配套的数字资源以二维码链接的形式呈现。利用手机微信扫码成功后提示微信登录,授权后进入注册页面,填写注册信息。按照提示输入手机号码,点击获取手机验证码,稍等片刻收到4位数的验证码短信,在提示位置输入验证码,再设置密码,选择相应专业,点击"立即注册",即注册成功。(若手机已经注册,则在"注册"页面底部选择"已有账号",进入"账号绑定"页面,直接输入手机号和密码登录)接着提示输入学习码,需刮开教材封面防伪涂层,输入13位学习码(正版图书拥有的一次性使用学习码),输入正确后提示绑定成功,即可查看二维码数字资源。手机第一次登录查看资源成功以后,再次使用二维码资源时,只需在微信端扫码即可登录进入查看。